SEA *of the* BEAR

SEA *of the* BEAR

Journal of a voyage to Alaska and the Arctic, 1921
by M. A. Ransom, Lieutenant Commander
United States Coast Guard (Retired)

with Eloise Katherine Engle

United States Naval Institute
Annapolis, Maryland

Preface

Some men join the Coast Guard to learn a trade, some enter the service hoping to make it a career; I enlisted for sheer adventure—and liked the life so much I stayed to make a career of it. For years before I entered the Coast Guard I had been thrilled by tales of the Revenue Cutter Service—their law enforcement patrols, and their rescues of ships and mariners in distress. Long before I wore a Coast Guard uniform, I knew about the famous Arctic cutters, the *Thetis, Snohomish,* and *Bear.* After World War I, when the Revenue Cutter Service became the Coast Guard, I determined to make a trip in the most famous of those ships, the *Bear.*

When I finally succeeded in becoming a member of the *Bear's* crew, it was said she was sailing on her last cruise. During that cruise I kept a diary, from which this book was later written, and used a drugstore-type Eastman Kodak to photograph many of the people and places depicted in these pages. But that was not the end of the *Bear;* she made many more trips to the Arctic and the Antarctic before she finally sank at sea in 1963.

Years after that first voyage into the Arctic, I finally wrote out the brief notes, the tales of old-timers, the thoughts and impressions I had recorded on that adventurous trip. The rough manuscript was polished into a concise, readable narrative by Eloise Engle, who knows Alaska and the Northwest and who shares my love for the sea.

Ships and seamen and life at sea have changed greatly since the times I wrote of, but the lure of the sea and the sense of adventure is still there for those who seek it, despite the technicians, scientists, and push-button experts who have replaced the horny-handed seamen and bull-voiced skippers of my time. I would say to any boy looking for an interesting, exciting future that the modern Coast Guard still offers this. For a career spiced, as mine was, with adventure, I would still say "join up." The *Bear* is gone, but there are other ships, and other seas.

M R Ranson

San Carlos, California
June 2, 1964

Foreword

The *Bear* has been many things to many men. To the many who sailed in her, or were rescued from starvation and death by her gallant crews, she is a fascinating legend. Each succeeding crew was left with a memory of a challenge accepted, a victory won. The Eskimos called her their "visiting angel."'

During her long life of ninety years the *Bear* roamed the polar seas, both north and south. Who can say which chapter was the most rewarding, the most spectacular? Each cruise meant something special to each crew.

Herein the author relates one chapter of the *Bear's* life—and what it meant to him. Along with his personal adventures, he describes some early history of Alaska and the Far North, as the *Bear* was a part of that history.

To me, the *Bear* is Admiral Byrd's Antarctic Expedition 1939-40. I answered the call for volunteers to go south with Byrd. The Navy had purchased the *Bear* for a modest sum, appropriated $100,000 to have her refitted, and placed her in commission. As a Lieutenant I was ordered to the *U.S.S. Bear* as navigator; her skipper was Lieutenant Commander Richard H. Cruzen, U. S. Navy. On this expedition, I first learned how to handle a ship in the ice, knowledge which stood me in good stead in later years. The memories are still vivid of the awesome icebergs, the penguins, and the killer whales. The friendships formed then, a quarter of a century ago, are lasting and dear to me.

The *Bear* rests on the bottom of the sea in the Atlantic Ocean. But to those of us who served in her, she still sails under full canvas like a phantom ship in the mists of yesterday.

George Dufek
Rear Admiral, U. S. Navy (Retired)

Director, The Mariners Museum
Newport News, Virginia

Table of Contents

Introduction

There was very little excitement along the water front when the barkentine *Bear* slid down the ways in 1874. To the Scottish workmen who had built her in the yard of Alexander Stephen and Sons, of Dundee, she was just another ordinary sail and steam-powered Arctic whaler, destined to the uneventful, humdrum life of all small ships at sea. But if ships have souls, as some sailors claim, then it was destined from the beginning that the *Bear's* proud spirit would make her known and loved by men in many oceans, for nearly a century.

For the first ten years of her life the *Bear* was an unknown member of the Newfoundland sealing fleet. Then, in 1884, the United States formed a rescue expedition into the Arctic to search for the Greely Expedition, which had been stranded in the Far North. The *Bear* was taken into the Navy for this job, and sailed north with the *Thetis* and the *Alert*. Two months later she found the pitiful survivors—the first of her many stirring Arctic rescues—and so became world famous.

In 1885 the ship was transferred to the Treasury Department for use in Alaskan waters, and thus began a forty-one-year career in the Alaskan Patrol which has never been surpassed.

The *Bear's* first skipper on the Alaskan Patrol was colorful "Hell Roarin' " Mike Healy, a dynamo of a man with an unpredictable temper. But Healy was a good skipper, and in the nine years he commanded the *Bear,* he and his ship became legend in the lusty, brawling Territory of Alaska.

Not the least of Healy's accomplishments was the importation of reindeer from Siberia to provide food for the natives who were never free of the threat of famine. As he reasoned, reindeer would also be an excellent source of clothing and transportation. The wisdom of this measure was dramatically demonstrated a few years later during the famous overland trek to save whalers marooned near Point Barrow, Alaska.

In the fall of 1897, eight whaling vessels and their crews totaling 275 men were trapped in an ice pack off remote Point Barrow. The *Bear* had only recently returned from her patrol duties, but at the order of the Secretary of the Treasury she prepared to go to the rescue on the first Arctic voyage ever attempted during the winter season.

The *Bear* was stopped by ice approximately eighty-five miles off Cape Nome, but before turning back she put ashore, on Nelson Island near Cape Vancouver, an overland party led by First Lieutenant D. H. Jarvis.

With dog teams, sleds, and guides, Jarvis and his companions made a 1,600 mile journey through frozen, trackless wilderness to Point Barrow. During the exhausting journey, they collected a herd of 450 reindeer which they drove ahead of them, reaching Point Barrow about three and one-half months later. To the despairing whalers, the arrival of the relief party was nothing short of a miracle. Healy's foresight had paid off, for the reindeer had indeed provided food, transportation, and clothing.

The *Bear's* duties in the Alaskan Patrol were many. She carried mail, government agents, supplies, and federal prisoners. Her deck often served as a court where justice was dispensed.

During World War I, the *Bear* served with the U. S. Navy. In 1929, she was decommissioned and turned over to the city of Oakland, California, for use as a maritime museum. It was at this time that she served as the set for the filming of Jack London's *Sea Wolf*.

The *Bear* was getting on in years now, but there were still great moments ahead for the stout old ship. In the early 1930's Rear Admiral Richard E. Byrd chose her for operating in ice in his Second Antarctic Expedition. Said the Admiral of her then, "She was respectably old when the *Oregon* raced around the Horn, but there was a fine and indestructible courage in her oak timbering with its sheathing of iron bark which age and rot could not corrupt. . . ." The *Bear* was refitted in Boston and under the command of Lieutenant (jg) Robert A. J. English, USN, reached the Bay of Whales and Little America in the latter part of January, 1934.

She sailed south again in the United States Antarctic Expedition of 1939-40. By May 16, 1941, she had completed her work in the Antarctic and was back in Boston.

By this time the shadow of World War II was already stretching over the United States. In 1941, shortly after her return from the Antarctic, the *Bear* was assigned to the Greenland Patrol operated by the U. S. Coast Guard. She took part in the capture of the Norwegian trawler *Buskoe,* which had been fitted out by the Germans to transmit weather reports and information on Allied ship movements. But the *Bear's* active service was nearly finished. In June, 1944, she was turned over to the Maritime Commission for sale.

For nearly twenty years the once proud old ship was almost forgotten. She seemed doomed to end her days in obscurity on a Nova Scotian beach. Finally, the *Bear* was purchased by Mr. Alfred M. Johnston of Villanova, Pennsylvania, who planned to turn her into a floating museum and restaurant in Philadelphia. Early in 1963, as she was being towed to Philadelphia, the *Bear* ran into a late winter storm ninety miles south of Cape Sable, Nova Scotia. In the thirty-foot seas, her towline parted, the square-rigged foremast snapped, the once tightly caulked seams opened, and the proud old *Bear* took a death list to starboard. The wind screamed through her rigging as she slowly turned over and went down. Her legendary career, spanning several generations, had finally ended, and the *Bear* took her resting place at the bottom of the sea, where most brave ships end. Along the water fronts, where the *Bear* had once been known, there were men who felt sad, yet relieved, at the loss of the old ship—a dull existence as a restaurant was not proper for her, they felt, and it was better she ended as she did.

The *Bear* will remain a shining symbol of courage and adventure, and her story will be told as long as men still sail the seas. *Sea of the Bear* is but one chapter in the long story of that gallant ship, as I saw it. I hope that in these pages she will live for others, as she always has for me.

M. A. R.

The Bear
was a ship men remembered.
She was a tough ship,
built for hard work.
She was known
in ports of the world
across two oceans.
In many seas men
remembered the Bear.

The Bear
was a tough ship. She outlived
the men who built her;
She outlasted Arctic ice,
gales in the Roaring Forties,
shipworm and reef.

The Bear
was a tough ship. For nearly
a century she outfought
the sea. In those
long years she took unnumbered
men to sea.
She trained them
in the mysteries of the wind,
the way of the wave,
the secrets of the sea.

The Bear
was more than a ship;
she was a school,
a home, a myth,
a tradition. Men never
forgot the Bear.

The Bear
lived in the sea,
and when her years ended, she died,
as do all great ships,
in the sea.

The Coast Guard cutter *Bear* lay at the dock, facing the channel, at Unalaska, Alaska, making ready for sea. From my vantage point aboard the *Unalga,* moored at the same dock, I could see that Boatswain Berg had cockbilled her foreyard. Now he yelled at the men who were heaving in slingloads of coal, "Get to the bunkers below!"

The hatch over the crew's quarters was off as the coal passed down through the berth deck. Soot would have been flying everywhere except for the drizzling rain which made black slime of it. The *Bear's* boats lay out on the dock, where they had been landed to keep them clear of the loading operation. Her poop deck was piled high with bags of coal, her well deck was littered with more coal and other gear. A partly grown hog grunted noisily in a corner, chewing happily on both garbage and coal.

I listened with envy as the *Bear's* pilothouse bells jangled. Then there came the blare of her steam whistle, testing for getting under way. On her afterdeck stood Quartermaster Black, a canny Scot, rainclothes pulled close around his face to keep out the drizzle. Louis Strauss, the Alaska Commercial Company agent, and other visitors from town were coming and going, saying their goodbyes to Captain Cochran, commanding officer of the *Bear.* Ironically, my own skipper was among the well-wishers.

Since I was supposed to be on watch, and because this was a familiar scene to all Coast Guardsmen on the Bering Sea Patrol, I forced myself to be sensible and to go about my duties. The *Bear* was just another ship, I told myself. And a "pierhead jump" or a transfer from one ship to another at this point was considered not only remote, but hopeless. It would be best to forget the idea and pretend that I had never asked for the transfer.

But would the nagging dream ever leave me? In all honesty, I knew it would not, for of all the ships that had flown the Stars and Stripes at their gaffs and won the affection of the men who walked their decks, the *Bear* stood first. Songs and poems had been written about her brave exploits and I knew them all. I had collected yarns about her—second, third, and fourth hand—always hoping that someday I might actually sail in her. I knew her background better than some people know their own kin.

Built in Dundee, Scotland, in 1874, she was neither beautiful nor young. As one of the last of the square-rigged, steam sailing ships, she had, by that day in 1921, put in forty-seven years of hard work in the icy waters of the North Atlantic and the Bering Sea.

As sailing ships went, her sails were small and few. Her once husky engine of 500 horsepower was meager and inadequate in terms of modern machinery. Under

3

steam, in fair weather, she could make nine knots. Under sail alone, she could log about eight. She was small: a scant 198 feet 6 inches from bow to stern and about 30 feet across her beam. Square-rigged on the foremast, fore-and-aft rigged on her main and mizzen masts, she had, through the years, maintained the good-luck omen of the shillings placed under the step of each mast by the workmen who built her. On each annual cruise to the North, she logged about 15,000 miles with the punctual regularity of a letter carrier.

My first knowledge of the *Bear* came in 1913 at Nushagak in Bristol Bay when I stood on the beach and watched the cutter *Thetis* steam in, carrying a federal court to try a man for murder. We had mistaken the *Thetis* for the *Bear,* and my shipmates at once launched a story-telling session of *Bear's* epic past. Then and there I determined to sail in that ship. A year later, in London, I met a man who had been rescued from a wrecked Arctic whaler by the *Bear.* Our excitement mounted as we discovered our mutual admiration for the gallant ship. I even caught myself pretending I had been one of her crew.

Some time later, when I boarded the U. S. Coast Guard cutter *Algonquin* at Gibraltar, I deliberately hunted out the men who could tell me about Alaska, the Bering Sea, and the *Bear.* More sea stories were swapped, and I eagerly hoisted them all aboard. It was exciting, and tantalizing, as if the hand of fate were gradually steering me nearer and nearer to my destiny.

Finally, in 1920, I went aboard the *Bear* for the first time, in Port Townsend, Washington, where she had been towed by the *Algonquin* after breaking down in Alaska. I admired her decks and her antiquated rigging, marvelled at her heavy oak timbers. The thick planking, sheathed with ironwood, seemed to have become more than mere protection for the men in her crew. Again, letting my fancy play havoc with reality, I imagined myself standing astride the bowsprit, gazing down into ice, imagined the crunching of the white stuff below me.

Looking down, I saw mounted under the bowsprit the carved figurehead, the bear which signified her name. Aloft, in the crow's nest, I could see the head and shoulders of some old salt, his eyes sweeping the horizon as they had done for many years over many seas. At that moment, he seemed not a man but a part of the ship, a symbol of that crystal northern world he could not forsake.

I pictured the *Bear* going about her duties in the frozen seas, butting at the ice with full steam, then backing down and ramming it again. And I fancied myself aboard her as she aided less hardy ships when they stove in under the grip of the ice or ripped out their keels on the rocks.

No, there would never again be such a ship as the *Bear.* An aura hovered over her which could be visualized only by a dreamer in some world of fantasy, something to be passed over by practical people. The truth struck me with full force. Then and there I asked for a transfer to the *Bear,* but as fate would have it, I was refused.

Well, if that was how it was to be, I would follow my love. I would sign on the *Unalga* and hope to make the switch to the *Bear* in Unalaska.

And that was where we were now, my dream and I, watching the *Bear* get ready for her next voyage. My heart was low, but not resentful, because I knew the Coast Guard could not cater exclusively to my personal desires. From the gray skies, the mist sifted down in melancholy stillness. Should I allow myself one more long look at the *Bear* as she moved nearer the minute when she would leave without me?

Before I could decide, the Officer of the Deck called me. "Ransom, I have something here for you."

Something for me?

He held out an envelope, sealed. I stared at it, ripped it open. Transfer orders! I read the first lines: "June 2, 1921. You are hereby ordered. . ."

To the U.S. Coast Guard cutter *Bear!*

Quartermaster Wickman stepped forward to relieve me of the watch. I saluted Lieutenant Coffin, Officer of the Deck, and then made tracks, fast.

Five minutes later I was aboard the *Bear,* seabag and all. The day was no longer gray to me. I was confused; I didn't even know where my bunk was located, but that was a small matter. I was actually on the *Bear* and going to sea with her. First off, Lieutenant Todd, Officer of the Deck of the *Bear,* told me to relieve a man named Black who was standing

4

The Bear *in Puget Sound, 1920.*

watch on the poop deck, for he was being transferred to the *Unalga* in my place.

As I tramped around on the bags of coal, I scarcely had time to look over my new ship before I heard the familiar order:

"Single up all lines!"

The boats were quickly hoisted in and triced to the strongbacks.

"All hands! Stand by to get under way!"

But where was my getting-under-way station? In the few minutes aboard my new ship I had lent a hand in a dozen places, in obedience to shouted orders. And then, "Ransom! Take the wheel."

The old wooden steering wheel on the flying bridge was nearly as high as my head, and certainly far older than I was. Rolling it right and left in response to gruff orders from the man on the bridge, I steered the ship out around Tuscarora Reef, scarcely noticing more than the village houses as they slipped past. Men in their grimy coaling clothes began squaring the yards, securing the boats for sea, battening the hatches. Now came the deck hose, jetting water around to wash away the coal grime, for though it was raining there was not enough falling to move the black filth.

I glanced around at my shipmates. They were strangers, yet before long I would know them well. Aboard this small ship in the Arctic there would be no secrets. We would know one another for our vices and virtues, our strengths and weaknesses, as we shared adventure and danger in the frozen North. For the Arctic is merciless and harsh and does not treat men gently. It is not a place for heroes, but for ordinary, determined, rugged men. Patience, endurance, and courage would be the most important qualities this crew could possess. I supposed they were there in abundance, for a ship is no greater than the men who sail her.

Long before I set foot aboard the *Bear* I had been told to look out for Cochran, the captain. "He's a tough customer, a bull walrus. Bold, gruff, severe, he's master of all around him." Yes, there he was, standing on the wing of the bridge in his massive reindeer-hide coat. He was shouting orders in a voice that resembled a foghorn. I vowed I would be on my guard while sailing on his ship but, at the same

Dead ahead was the six-masted barkentine City of Sydney.

time, I pledged my complete respect for this master of my destiny in the months to come.

We passed out of Dutch Harbor entrance, by the spit. On our left I could see the old buildings which housed the defunct Udakta post office. On the right again, I had a last look at Priest Rock, dim and eerie in the misty air. Soon on the port bow appeared a shadowy headland—Cape Cheerful. Now, what kind of a joke was that supposed to be? Cheerful!

I rolled the wheel and flicked the rain out of my eyes, the better to see the compass in the binnacle in front of me. The sea beneath us was a dreary, greenish-gray color, but the rain beating down gave it a deceptively quiet look. Automatically, I relaxed my stance and allowed my sea legs to give and take with the gentle rolling of the ship. It was good to feel the ship come alive, to hear the creak and rattle and clatter of the boat blocks as she strained against the waves. The hog had given up chewing on chunks of coal and was now complaining loudly. I smiled to myself as I remembered the old saying, "Independent as a hog on ice. . . ."

The ship was not alone on the ocean as yet. Dead ahead was the six-masted barkentine *City of Sydney* which had brought coal to Unalaska, while off in another direction was the fisheries tender *Eider*. Steaming into the harbor that we had just left was the cutter *Algonquin*. How often that friendly, gallant ship had figured in my destiny! I wondered if any of her crew remembered our conversations at Gibraltar and how I had wanted duty on the *Bear*.

Also at anchor at Dutch Harbor were the codfish schooners *Galilee* and *Maweema* and, as I watched them fade into the mist, I thought what a strange world men of the sea live in. Ships, we know, have souls and personalities. Some we like, some we do not, just as with people. Some ships are good, others give nothing but trouble. Yet, we care very much when one of "our" ships meets disaster, for often a part of ourselves goes down with her. We would never again see her sailing past, her sails filling with the wind, her bow dipping into the foaming waves.

The *Bear* stood out to sea now. Ashore, on the starboard beam, we could see the graveyard, reminding us of the flu epidemic of 1919. The *Bear* had

We saw the graveyard of the Greek Orthodox Church.

arrived in the midst of the tragedy and the ship's doctor had worked round the clock, ministering to the ailing Eskimos, but fifty of them had died. Squinting hard against the rain and mist, I could barely make out the shapes of the four little cannon on the village green, left there in 1867 by the departing Russians.

The scene fascinated me, as did the view of "Molly's House" as we moved along. These were things I hoped would never be dulled by time. I was determined to keep a diary about the places I visited and the people I met. I would begin with Tom Moran, who for years was the Alaska Commercial Company's watchman at Dutch Harbor.

Knowing my interest in history, Tom Moran had taken me out to examine relics of the past—the old bar of Ye Baranof Inn, all that was left when the frontier hotel burned, standing open out in wind and weather and turning white with time; a rusting blubber trypot left by some forgotten whaler; the otter boat seized from a Japanese sealer; the flagpole made from the topmast of the cutter *Perry* which had been wrecked on St. Paul Island in 1910; the dust-cluttered room which had been the post office in the company building, and the heaps of old papers lying around on the floor. There, one day, Tom picked up three old journals.

"Take 'em if you want 'em," he said, handing them to me. "I'm going to burn 'em anyways."

Here were the daily recordings of the trading company's agent, which he had begun at the turn of the century and continued to 1919. Did he not realize that the rich history of Alaska was bound up in the simple data of the hundreds of ships that came to call? Warships, revenue cutters, sealers, salmon packets, codfishermen, and merchant ships—why they were there and what they did. The notes told of shipwrecks, belching volcanos, and scandals and, strangely enough, the first entry was about the *Bear* in 1902. No, I doubt if the old man knew how I would treasure the weathered pages of the journals in the years to come.

His eyes crinkled, and he grinned as he watched me leaf through one of the books. "Maybe you were born curious, eh?"

"I guess so," I replied, holding tight to the books. "But it seems to me that if you don't know what has happened before, then what happens now doesn't make much sense."

The old man pursed his lips in thought, shrugged his shoulders, and started back towards the house. "Well, if you want to hear some yarns, I've got plenty to tell ya."

And so he did. On rainy days he loved to sit with his heels cocked on the edge of a table, behind which was a cabinet filled with blue Delft chinaware. The dishes had been brought there in the 1890's by Molly Brown, wife of the trading company's agent. The gingerbread-adorned cottage, which had once been her home and where Moran now lived, had been erected specially for her by the company. She was the daughter of President Garfield, and everybody talked about Molly Garfield who had braved the wilds of the new territory of Alaska to be with her husband. The house became the gathering place for officers from the revenue cutters and the naval vessels that frequented the port during the Seal Island dispute.

Molly would be talked about even now on the bridge of the *Bear,* for Captain Cochran, as a young lieutenant, had often been a visitor at her cottage. Molly was, in fact, a legend. Do you know about Molly Garfield? Have you ever been to Molly's house? Have you ever seen Molly's Dutch chinaware?

My musings were interrupted by the call, "Make ready to set sails!"

I was glad to be on the wheel at that moment because setting and taking in sails aboard a steam vessel is hard, treacherous work for those who go aloft. Smoke and gases from the ship's fires billowed out of the smokestack to blind and choke the men as they worked high on the yards. Soot-covered, they were forced to claw at the ropes and canvas, soggy and slippery with rain and blackened with grime. The rolling of the ship along with the cold breeze tried the muscles and nerves of the men on the yards. Carelessness or bad luck could mean a fatal plunge into the icy sea below.

But Captain Cochran, an old-fashioned sailor, ordered the sails set whenever the wind was fair. And he required that the lookout always stand his watch in the crow's nest. That watch, though often a physical hardship, could be what the man made of it. He could spend his watch being miserable, or he could glory in the view of faraway horizons. He could perch there, high above the sea, to look downward at the deck of the heaving ship, as she ran before her tossing wake, and almost forget his troubles.

But let him not become so lost in fancy as to forget his job. For Captain Cochran was not prone to tolerate daydreams that might gather like cobwebs in a boy's thoughts. The safety of the *Bear* and her crew came first. The cry of "Ice ahead!" had better come from the crow's nest rather than the bridge, or disciplinary action would be taken.

With the wind in her sails now, the *Bear* skimmed proudly over the waves. She was bound again for Nome, the Arctic Ocean, the Yukon, and Siberia, with Demarcation Point as her final destination. What adventures would she find? What dangers would she encounter in the frozen wastelands of the North? This time, I was going along to find out.

Chapter Two : Alaska Means Gold and Ice

Alaska: That distant land, new to me, toward which the *Bear* now pointed her prow. What would it be like?

What did thousands of miles of wild country mean to the United States and to the world? What was the *Bear's* mission? How would we on the *Bear* help her carry it out?

As I thought about these questions, I was thankful for what Tom Moran called my "curiosity." Mainly, my interest in history was directed towards the sailing aspects of the Alaskan waters, yet I knew that the welfare of the land and its people were of great concern to us. In my mind's eye, I reviewed what I knew about Alaska.

I knew that Alaska extended from latitude 51 to 72 degrees North and from 130 degrees West to 173 degrees East longitude. In an area of 590,000 square miles, the 1920 census found only 55,036 people and most of them were Eskimos.

I knew that Alaska was purchased from Russia for $7,200,000 right after the Civil War, in 1867. In those times the United States cared little, and knew nothing, about the frozen insular domain. There were too many problems at home then, and too little time to worry about a far-off territory, separated from our country by the wilds of Canada, and offering little of value except for the sea otter pelts.

Land was plentiful and free to the taker, a couple of centuries ago, when Peter the Great sent an expedition to Kamchatka and to the dreary wastes beyond in search of territory and riches for the Czars.

Vitus Bering, a Dane in the service of the Czar, led the expedition. He and his lieutenant, Chirikof, penetrated as far as southeastern Alaska. Bering died and was buried on one of the lonely islands he had visited. The desolate sea between Alaska and Siberia was named after him. Chirikof gave his name to an island off the southwest peninsula of the Alaskan mainland.

In 1786, Pribilof came to the foggy seas and found the fabulous seal colonies on the islands which now bear his name. By his discovering where seals live and breed, he opened the door to the pelagic sealers who filled the region with international strife for more than a century before settlement was made.

After the Russian explorers came the fur traders, who moved as far south as San Francisco Bay, collecting a fortune in sea-otter skins. They built a post near the spot where the Russian River flows out of the California mountains into the Pacific Ocean. A few battered churches mark where Russian Orthodox priests followed the traders.

Fortunately, they did not maintain their stand there for a number of reasons. For one thing, easterners were moving west and the Spanish were coming up from the south. Since the Russians were more interested in exploiting the land than settling it, they left. St. Michael still stood as an aged blockhouse, reminding us of Russian influence there. On the greensward at Unalaska, a number of tiny cannon told of the other contacts. All along the way, remnants of decayed log forts reminded us of Czarist cruelty to the Eskimos in days past. Little churches of the Russian, Greek Orthodox creed stood battered but firm in their cold foundations.

Meanwhile, Captain Cook, the great English explorer, swung through the south seas and swept along the Alaskan shore to the Arctic Ocean on his memorable surveying expedition. Vancouver followed soon after, laying the foundation for British interest in the rich new areas.

And the United States was expanding. Westward came the whalemen, following the herds from Cape Horn to the Arctic through the same seas the Russians had explored, coasting the same shores where Bering had started Russian settlements.

The Czar wanted badly to be rid of his unprofitable "Russian America," but the United States was not eager for the purchase. Months of dickering were to elapse before settlement was made. Secretary of State Seward, who favored the purchase, reminded his opponents that the Czar had assisted the Union cause during the war. Could we not take Alaska off their hands as a gesture of thanks? Then, too, the Monroe Doctrine was at stake since a European power owned the territory. It would be best to ward off trouble before it began.

Finally, at 4 o'clock in the morning of March 30, 1867, Secretary of State Seward and Baron Edouard de Stoeckl signed the treaty assigning to the United States what was referred to by Americans as "Seward's Folly." Alaska could well have been a financial blunder had it not been for the roving whalemen, the plainsmen, and the men moving westward in search of gold. After the Civil War, restless men were looking towards the Far North as a means of making a quick stake. Eventually, some of them did find riches, in whale oil, fur, gold, and salmon.

Alaska at the time of purchase was a mystery. Although the coastline was charted somewhat, the interior was a geographical blank. There was but one

An old Russian blockhouse still stood at St. Michael.

lighthouse, no buoys, and no beacons, for 35,000 miles of lonely coast.

Soon the Coast Guard Cutter *Lincoln* was sent to Sitka and the Aleutian Islands to locate the most valuable channels for commerce, to spot the most probable haunts for smugglers, and to line up suitable points for customs houses, lighthouses, and coaling stations.

Before long, cutters of the Alaskan service were cruising along the coast, sending boat expeditions up rivers and into territories previously unknown even to Yukon traders.

The cutters carried government inspection parties, army engineers, army signal corpsmen, and members of various other governmental bureaus. There was fascinating and often dangerous work for everyone in this virgin territory. Even the floor of the Bering Sea was explored and charted. Volcanic in origin, depths reached over 2,000 fathoms in places and then, suddenly, far out to sea, dangerous shoals appeared, which could easily smash hapless vessels to bits in a storm-tossed sea. Each cutter kept her lead line going during every moment she was under way north of Akutan Pass, not only for her own protection but for aid to the U. S. Hydrographic Office chart makers.

Exploring was only one of many responsibilities of the Coast Guard cutters. By special law, certain designated Coast Guard officers were permitted to administer oaths in Alaska. Federal law had to be upheld in the new territory and it became the duty of the Coast Guard to carry the famous "floating court." Each spring, a federal judge and other necessary officials would board a cutter and travel from port to port, bringing courthouse and justice to communities that were too small or inaccessible to permit permanent courts.

Cutters such as the *Lincoln, Wolcott, Corwin, Bear, Unalga, Haida, Shoshone, Rush, Northland, Spencer, Duane,* and *Alert* became the symbols of law and order in Alaska. The word soon got around that when the cutters dropped their hooks off Nome, the rough and ready miners had better toe the mark.

From the very beginning of their duty in Alaska, cutters made thrilling excursions into ice packs to aid ships of the American whaling fleet. Rescue after rescue was performed under almost unsurmountable hardships. Thousands of lives were saved by the gallant mercy ships.

The cutters also aided the natives with food, medicines, and medical help in villages stricken with influenza, measles, or famine. To the Eskimos, the *Bear* was known as the "Visiting Angel."

The Coast Guard was delegated to protect the seals in the Pribilof Islands from poachers who would have slaughtered the herds to extinction. They supervised the killing of whales, enforced fishing regulations, and protected the salmon by seizing illegal fish traps.

It seemed their jobs were endless, yet the dedicated "icemen" who spent their lives in this service would have had it no other way. *Semper Paratus*—Always Prepared. That was our motto.

In the sea of the *Bear,* we had to be prepared at all times for any job or peril that came our way. Now I saw that our immediate peril was Nunivak Island off the mouth of the Kuskokwim River. There the sea shoaled to five fathoms and the *Bear* swung off shore to deeper, safer water.

The temperature hung just above freezing. The water temperature readings taken in the engine room did not satisfy the Captain. He'd had too many years in the ice to take chances. Soon he called the quartermaster. "Do you see this bucket with a thermometer in it? Every half hour I want it filled with sea water for five minutes. We will practice this while under way for the rest of the season."

In addition to taking water temperature, soundings would be made every half hour, sometimes every fifteen minutes. In close waters, I would soon learn that a man would be stationed in the chains, *constantly* heaving the lead.

Now the temperature dropped, in the air, in the sea. So the Arctic made itself known—we were coming to ice and it was as though a mesmerizing cloud had settled over our minds. Each man, I guessed, felt his own personal reaction to the white spots which began to appear on the northern horizon. I do not think there was fear, but, more likely, respect for the awesomely inhospitable waste of ice we were about to enter. I remembered the description of sea ice by Sir John Ross, ". . . Sea ice is stone, a floating rock in

13

the stream, a promontory or an island when aground, not less solid than if it were a land of *granite.*"

Soon after we sighted ice, I noticed that Captain Cochran had stopped to talk with John Lidmann, a boatswain's mate with whom I had spent some time earlier in the trip. Seated on a heap of old sails in the forepeak, John was sewing canvas with the steady hand of long experience. I wondered what he and the Captain were talking about. Was John recalling the old days when he'd been a greasy whaleman aboard the *Jeannie* when the *Bear* had rescued them at Point Barrow in 1897-98? Or were they reminiscing about John's twenty-five years spent aboard the cutters *Thetis* and *Bear*?

John and the Captain were "old cronies," old ship-mates. They both knew the North as a newcomer could not. John's judgment of things pertaining to ice and the Arctic was sound, and I had a feeling it often reached into the thoughts and judgment of the man who had to make the decisions. I supposed these icemen characterized the soul of the *Bear* as well as any men could. Yet I would soon learn how diversified we all were.

Now the ship began passing isolated fields of flat ice, floating in a confused state with a slow, sluggish motion. With each mile, the floes grew larger and more numerous. Soon, ice covered our watery world, and the ship turned and twisted among the floes.

The man in the crow's nest huddled inside his barrel, keeping a sharp eye out for the lines of darker water which indicated the path the *Bear* should take. But the watery leads grew fewer. Solid ice loomed ahead. The ship crashed into it, pushing sheets a foot thick helter-skelter. Sometimes the stuff was two or three feet thick in places. I knew from reading that the biggest floes would not exceed a thickness of fifteen feet. But—fifteen feet of solid granite! The ice stiffened and the ship stuck fast, but not for long. Backing away, we began to cautiously steam along the edge, looking for leads to drive into.

For miles the ship zigzagged until the lookout in the crow's nest shouted, "Lead to the starboard!"

A long, dark streak showed us the way in. The ship butted forward, inch by inch. The *Bear* creaked and groaned as the sullen pressure ridges closed in on

The lookout kept a sharp eye out for leads through the ice.

her. The crew cursed the shrill, angry winds that swept off the fields of ice.

I thought of Chuck Speechley, sweating away down in the black grime of the engine room, coaxing the *Bear* to full steam. As a shellback, an old-timer who had been to sea for fifteen or twenty years, he knew ships, all kinds of ships. He had sailed in them, and watched them, and could name them afar off as easily as one named a friend across the street.

"That's the *Star of India,*" Chuck had told Lidmann, as he pointed to a ship in Unimak Pass. It was one of the famous "Star" boats belonging to the Alaska Packers fleet. I had seen them, making a forest of masts, where they lay in Oakland. Chuck knew them, and their history—that the *Star of India* had once been named *Euterpe,* that the *Star of Alaska* had once been named *Balclutha.*

Although they carried nothing but fish in their holds, and their crew was largely Chinese and Japanese cannery workers, the "Star" boats were beautiful to see. They sailed north from San Francisco in April of each year, a swarm of white-winged craft, to load canned salmon in Bristol Bay. One day in 1918, there had been eight "Star" ships within a mile or so of each other, waiting for a fair wind to take them through Unimak Pass. They all returned to San Francisco in September. The Alaska Packers started their "Star" fleet after the turn of the century when they bought four ships which once belonged to the famous line of "Corry's Irish Stars"—*Star of France, Star of Bengal, Star of Italy,* and *Star of Russia.* As they added *Star of Iceland, Star of Alaska, Star of Finland,* and others, the list of "Stars" grew until there were nineteen of them.

While Chuck Speechley had been learning ships, he also learned about ice. He was one among us who knew the Arctic well. This was his ship and he would continue to sweat and strain until the crisis was past.

But the ice was too much for the old ship. Try as they might, the black gang could not get up enough power to push her through. So we lay and waited.

Night came on, yet at that season of the year night was only half-darkness and half-light in a starless sky. For want of anything better to do, I made notes in my diary. My closest observation concerned the crew and the firm, strict discipline which held us together, making us a part of the ship itself. This was a neces-

15

The "Star" boats formed a forest of masts.

sary thing, because many of the men were in some ways a product of those restless times.

The end of the war left, all around the country and at every seaport, countless men who, for the moment, were jobless and undirected. Some of these had signed on with the *Bear*. Then there were the boys, too young to go off to war, who now longed to set out on some kind of adventure. We had sneak thieves, troublemakers, and lazy ones who were always trying to dodge duty. And we had our share of blowhards who always had a bigger story to tell than the last one.

Two of our crewmen had just returned from service in the Army, in Siberia. The carpenter's mate had sailed around the world in 1907 with the Great White Fleet, when Theodore Roosevelt showed the world our American naval strength.

Another of the men had sailed in the brig *Carnegie* from Dutch Harbor to Australia. And then there was the young fisherlad from Grimsby, England, who wanted to impress me with the hardships of the trawlerman's life up around the Iceland banks. He quit the fishboats, started out to see the world, was stranded in San Francisco, and shipped in the *Bear* to get his bellyful of an entirely different kind of ship. Having come from a family of old-fashioned sailing ship people, with the lore of the British seamen in his soul, he was determined to carry on the tradition. Now, as the *Bear* waited in the cold, half-light of night, I could hear him singing:

"Haul up the clew garnet, let fly tack and sheet,
From Ushant to Scilly is forty-five leagues . . ."

I braced myself and waited for other songs that were due to follow. Surely our commissary steward, Paddy, who was ex-British Army, would favor us with "Shake hands with sister Susie upon the garden gate."

There it was, accompanied by a harmonica. Heavily-booted toes tapped in rhythm. Some men laughed, others kept quiet. In a crew such as this, there would always be many points of view and opinions.

The newcomers to ship life voiced their thoughts mainly about their bellies and the harshness of living conditions. "The food is no good," they grumbled.

"What, salt beef again?" Or, the next day, the same man said, "Don't we ever get anything but reindeer meat?"

A fellow complainer chimed in, "I'm sick of canned foods; I want fresh vegetables."

And they mumbled bitterly about having to clean up an aged ship that seemed never to be quite clean enough as there was always a musty smell in the dark corners. There were too many hours on watch for the deck force who stood watch and watch (four hours on—four hours off) from the time the vessel got under way until she came to anchor in some safe roadstead. And they could look forward to standing watch and watch even at anchor when we found ourselves in exposed places, which would be nearly all summer.

The newcomers were forever grumbling for more and better of everything. The water supply was too meager, the faucets in the washroom too few, and the amount that flowed from each too little. Water rations were a thing for the ancients, not a modern ship. Drinking from scuttlebutts in the corner of the berth deck was good enough, but the water should be more plentiful and fresher tasting.

"Now, ain't that jes' too bad?" growled one of the oldtimers. "Seems to me you ought to go aft and tell the 'old man' your troubles."

But nobody went, either for fear of being laughed at or given a reprimand.

Old John Lidmann put the grumblers in their places by recalling the old days. "You think you've got it rough? Why, you don't even know the meaning of being a sailor. I've sailed on ships where the 'chief crusher' poured a bucketful of water in a wooden tub for twenty men to wash their faces in. We got our drinking water from a bucket that hung from a nail in the overhead beam."

Chuck Speechley chimed in. "How would you lubbers like to wash your clothes in a mixture of urine and grease for soap and then rinse them out in salt water? Or better still, you could drag them astern on the end of a line."

Such talk soon drove the young gripers into embarrassed silence.

And then there was the matter of discipline which showed itself very early in the trip. I allowed myself to muse about this as I scribbled notes in my diary.

The way I saw it, every time a young man—commissioned or enlisted—goes to sea, he becomes subject to regulations and discipline. He begins to like or dislike the restrictions around him by nursing ideas of what he might do to change or improve the setup; and he swears that if he ever finds himself in a position of authority, he will change things. For the better, of course.

Some men do arrive at that position and they begin pecking away at the rules men have lived by for ages. But changes made by these reformers are not what they imagined when they first began thinking about them. For, in the meantime, they have found that those rules may be hard to live with but much harder to live without.

This lesson had been learned long ago by Captain Cochran. It was a lesson that one of my shipmates, LaRue, knew deep in his heart was a good one, though he still spouted notions of how to change it. He, like many others, wanted to season the pudding to suit his own taste.

Yes, there were many on board who cherished their opinions, each expressing them in his own way, some aloud, some by inward reflection. But none was ever able to change the basic concept that such regulations were good for the ship. And it was soon learned that nobody seasoned the pudding served by Captain Cochran.

Backing up the Captain right down the line was Ralston, our Master-at-Arms, an ex-Marine, with a voice like thunder and powerful hands as large as hams. "Out in the Philippines I used to be one of a firing party who sent volleys over the graves of departed buddies," he told us once. We never learned how those buddies got killed, but the tale had a somewhat sobering effect on would-be roustabouts. We were convinced Ralston would do the same for us if it became necessary.

Waiting to work free of the hard, blue-white ice required patience and endurance. The crew, though heavily clothed, constantly ran the risk of frozen eyelids, fingers, toes, and cheeks as they performed their shipboard chores. Waiting in the harsh cold was depressing and numbing. Time seemed to stand still. Minds dulled and conversation lagged. Yet, strangely enough, there was optimism. "Keep a sharp eye!" the Captain called to the man in the crow's nest.

And then it happened! A breeze sprang up from the southwest, then freshened. "That's what we've been waiting for. And high time, too." The Captain's voice rose with anticipation. "Wind from that quarter will start a swell in the open water to the southward."

As if the sea had heard and answered, we heard rumblings over the ice, then sharp crackling all around the barrier ahead. The entire ship tensed as the crunching rose to a thundering roar.

"There she goes!" the lookout called jubilantly.

A long lead of dark water opened wide in the ghostly whiteness. The *Bear* backed, then under full steam rammed into the opening. She plowed ahead, slowly, painstakingly. Aloft, the masthead lookout told us that the lead widened in and across the vast field that had held us back.

Although we could not see Nome as yet, we knew that it was near.

All day we drove on while the great white barrier gradually loosened around us. Open water areas increased. The streak which was the horizon became sharper. Finally we saw it as a line of low hills behind the straggling town. Through the bleak mist we could see the soft green tundra which covered the hills contrasting with the low buildings near the waterfront.

Nome at last! The *Bear* anchored in an open area of water several miles off shore. I noted the date in the ship's log—June 7, 1921. The *Bear* had taken just five days to sail from Unalaska to Nome.

Midnight. Nome lay in the twilight beyond the white streak which marked the shoreline to the north of us. Were I an artist, I would have been tempted to sketch the staunch figure of John Lidmann, standing his watch, outlined against the maze of stays, halyards, and fishfalls which spread out like giant spiderwebs around him, for this was a scene that excited all the senses. Behind the town the sky was aglow, for in this strange land, the sun set in the North. Down now, it sent up a pale shimmering light over the cloudless sky. As "night" wore on, it would travel all the way around the horizon, with no curtain of darkness to blot out the scene. Not a breath of air stirred in this exquisite setting of solitude. Even the seabirds, noisy in their incessant chatter during the day, had gone somewhere to pass a few quiet hours.

19

But there were noises—ominous, melancholy sounds which seemed to embody the loneliness of the man standing watch on the bow of the *Bear*. In the windless night, the heavy swell put up a strong surf which beat its lonely chant against the ice floes grounded on the beach.

To this accompaniment, the *Bear* heaved and creaked as she lay at anchor in the unprotected waters. Off to seaward, we could see great white cakes, some larger than a football field, others but small porridge ice, constantly in motion. The big cakes lumbered like awkward giants, while the little ones danced in this constant agitation.

Men experienced in Arctic ice—icemen, we called them—knew that this was the beginning of the breakup of the long northern winter. It could mean danger, but, true to our motto, we of the *Bear* were prepared with whatever precautions we were capable of taking. We could not allow ourselves to be hypnotized by the beauty of this Arctic night.

For one thing, sea watches had been continued though the *Bear* had long been at anchor, and the cable was kept at short stay, ready to heave in if need be. The man in the crow's nest kept a constant eye out for trouble, while the duty officer leaned over his charts in the pilothouse, patiently plotting our future courses. The loiterers played cards under the shelter deck, quietly, but with a tense air, as the distant surf beat against the icy beach and the ship rolled beneath them.

As the night crept on, I began to feel uneasy about the rolling of the vessel and the confused movement of the ice. I wondered if John Lidmann, watching in the bow, felt this same premonition of danger. It was impossible to know, for he seemed not to move a muscle as he stood with legs spread wide, holding onto the forestay with one hand as he peered out over the drifting ice. Calm, stoic, dependable, and wise—that was John.

Suddenly the crow's nest watch shouted down, "Iceberg bearing down on the bowsprit!"

The men on deck hugged the rail to watch the monstrous floe, bigger than the *Bear,* move closer and closer. The swell swung it first one way, then another.

"It could fetch up athwart the jibboom," the young English fisherlad said huskily, trying to conceal his concern. "I say we'd better do something."

The Bear *heaved and creaked in the ice.*

No one bothered to answer. We each had our private thoughts about this cold, silent enemy that might well do the ship deadly damage.

John Lidmann grasped an oar, climbed to the jibboom end and thrust vainly at the ice, while others shouted and cursed.

Slowly the floe moved sideways and around, sidling along the side of the ship, still threatening the *Bear*. If it hit her underwater hull, it could tear a gaping hole and send the *Bear* plunging to the bottom in a matter of minutes. No human could live long in these frigid Arctic waters.

"On deck the watch!" Lidmann yelled.

Men came running with oars, boathooks, anything that had length and strength. Now all hands pushed with their full weight against the mass which slowly worked aft at each rise and fall of the water. Officers appeared from the wardroom. Berg made his way up from steerage and Captain Cochran, pajama-clad but wearing his tan and white reindeer coat, looked out the cabin hatch. With a calm air he watched the struggle against the cold, white enemy. He leaned down and patted his collie puppy, Thor, as if to say, "Don't worry. We'll look out for you."

The crew cheered as the iceberg slid free of the *Bear*. Some men stared after the white monster as though they still distrusted it. Others slumped their tired shoulders and began putting gear back in place. One glance at the Captain's face told me we were not out of danger yet. His cigar was clenched tightly in his teeth and his voice was gruff. "Check the anchor chain. Keep steam on the throttle. We may have to move out if the ice gets worse!"

But for that night the *Bear* was troubled no more. Captain Cochran went back to the comfort of his bed, the duty officer returned to his charts, the watch to the shelter of the overhang of the shelter deck, the loiterers resumed their card game, and John again took station out on the forecastlehead to peer into the softly lit sky as if nothing had happened. But not quite, for Thor, the Captain's pup, had become frightened and sick during the excitement and the struggle with the ice. I heard him whimpering pitifully while the Captain, so gruff and stern with men, soothed him in gentle tones, "Come on, boy. That's a good dog. Here, have a bit of supper. . . ."

I first met Thor on my second morning aboard the *Bear*. As I climbed over the coal sacks on the poop deck on the way aft to take a sounding, I was surprised by a sharp bark, followed by a tremulous little growl which was not unfriendly but rather quizzical. Rounding the deckhouse, I came face to face with a collie pup tied to the turnbuckle of the mizzen backstay. Captain Cochran, on the bridge, watched impassively as I patted the dog on the head and scratched the fuzzy ears. I wondered even then how this supersensitive young dog would fare during the rough and rugged voyage he was only just beginning.

As time passed, we noticed that Thor did not grow as fast as he should have. His nose reached out and his tail got bushier, but his fur was always scraggly and not thick enough to protect him from the cold. Soon he developed an aversion to the sea and nobody could do a thing about it. Doctoring, dieting, and all the care bestowed upon him did no good. He lost his appetite and got spells of distemper. He crouched in terror of the screaming gulls overhead and trembled at the approach of people, except for those who cared for him. Each morning when the deck force began to wash down the deck, he took off in fright toward the safety of the cabin hatch because of his violent fear of water.

Poor Thor! He had the best accommodations we could offer, but it was soon apparent that he would never become a seasoned sailor. The poop deck extended aft for a quarter of the length of the vessel, raised up about four feet above the level of the main deck. This area, reserved for official purposes, was known as "officer country," or the quarterdeck. This was the place in which Thor was permitted to play. This was also a place that had to be kept immaculate, and this was the place where Thor always got sick.

Cleaning up the quarterdeck became the job of the boatswain's mate of the watch. Lidmann provided a canvas bucket and a broom. The duty of knowing when to use them devolved on the quartermaster of the watch. Between looking for land or ice, or telltale white flicks of shoal waters around the horizon, or taking soundings, or writing the rough log, or taking salt water temperatures and noting the weather, the quartermaster also had to keep his eye on the quarterdeck. When Thor happened to have his usual difficulties, some one would call out, "Dog on the Q. D.!"

Then came a scramble as the detailed man grabbed the bucket, dipped up some seawater, and began scrubbing. The whole performance became a joke among the crew forward. But there was always sympathy for Thor.

Day or night, at anchor or in a rolling seaway, when the cry "Dog on the Q.D." came, everyone knew what had happened. The call came to be as much a part of the ship's routine as "All hands!" or "Away the whaleboat!" and was as smartly acted upon.

Only one man did not like Thor—Boatswain's Mate Crandall. He was one of those men the war and the seaman's strike had brought into the service. He did his work well, was never late for muster, and never got into trouble. But he was unhappy. It was rumored that he had been in the Navy, had sailed in sailships a time or two. And he hated the "bucket brigade."

"Wonder what's eating him," I remarked to Lidmann one night when we were ashore at Nome. Nome had no sidewalks then, just a muddy corduroy road along which we saw Crandall walking disconsolately.

"Who can say?" replied Lidmann. "He might be happier drinking hot sake in some Yokohama saloon, or in Panama Kelly's bar. Maybe he'd rather be in the Chesapeake, and old Baltimore."

"Do you think he'll ever be happy on the *Bear?*" I asked, as we followed the sounds of a tinkling piano into a music hall.

"No, but you're going to find misfits wherever you sail. You watch, Crandall will come aboard tonight, sullen and unhappy as usual."

And so he did. He never told anyone what troubled him. He simply nursed his feelings in silence by hating the Captain's dog.

23

Ahoy! Ship standing in!" It was LaRue shouting from the crow's nest.

"Can you identify her?" I called back, ready to enter the name in the log.

Soon the old ex-whaler was forging toward us through the ice. It was clear that they had urgent business with the *Bear*, for the *Herman* had hardly dropped anchor close aboard before her Swedish skipper, Captain Pedderson, and a big burly stranger clothed in a heavy reindeer coat climbed into their whaleboat and rowed over to the *Bear*.

Captain Cochran waited by the rail as they climbed the accommodation ladder, saluted their greetings, and stamped their mukluked feet on our deck.

"Welcome aboard," Captain Cochran said. "Come along for a cup of hot Joe?"

"No time for that!" The stranger shook his shaggy, bearded head. "I've got to have help right away. It's your duty to supply it."

"Ours?" asked the "Bull Walrus," already bristling over what sounded like an assumption of his authority.

"Yah!" The stranger pulled back his furred hood. He was the famous Norwegian explorer-adventurer, Roald Amundsen. His had been the first voyage in the *Gjoa* across the top of the northern world. Following this was the race toward the South Pole. His wanderings were legend among icemen.

He spoke in a heavy accent. "We have been working on the experiment that will change history." I watched the steam of his breath as he explained excitedly, "One of the greatest. . ."

"What happened?" Captain Cochran was anxious to skip the histrionics. "The last news I heard was that you had taken the schooner *Maud* up North and set her adrift to test the flow of the Arctic currents."

Captain Pedderson lit his pipe. I thought I noticed a small twinkle of amusement. "The currents flowed one way, the plans, another."

"Yah!" Amundsen scowled. Were they daring to question the experience and ability of such a giant as he? Well, he would settle that right now. "Sure the *Maud* jammed in the ice near Cape Serdze, Siberia. We would have been helpless until summer. But great seamanship and a hardworking crew brought her down the coast to Whalen, just north of East Cape in the Arctic Ocean."

"That is where we found her," Captain Pedderson said in agreement.

"Now you know I did not desert my ship. I am here for help. I want you to take the *Bear* two hundred miles to where the *Maud* lies. . . ." Amundsen all but shook a gloved fist in Captain Cochran's face. We in the crew held our breaths, wondering what would become of our plans for the summer. The *Bear* had

25

many stops to make and a tight schedule to keep. But beyond that, we were fascinated by the clash of these two bristling, powerful icemen. Even Thor perked up his ears as he stared down from the quarterdeck.

Captain Cochran narrowed his eyes and glanced at first one man, then the other. "Any lives in danger?"

"No. But. . . ."

"Captain Pedderson, is the *Maud* in danger of breaking up?"

"Oh, she'll be all right. Summer is coming on."

"Well, then," Captain Cochran said, very matter-of-factly, "I am afraid you will have to wait for us to haul you out of your predicament. The *Bear* will be in that region in due time."

Amundsen balled his gloved fist and slammed it into the palm of his other hand. "But I want to get out now! We have important work to do. We can't wait!"

"I'm afraid you'll have to. The ice in the Bering Strait is still jammed tight. We could get through under our own power but it would not be feasible for us to tow you back unless there was an emergency." The men glared in silence for a moment or two. "Now, will you have some coffee before you leave?"

Why were we here? What was it all about? Strange how these thoughts took hold of me as we lay at anchor on the top of the world. I still had not gotten used to my good fortune of being aboard the *Bear* and until now had not indulged myself the time to ask these questions. "Just be glad that you are here," had been my motto. Yet, this day, standing anchor watch with nothing but swells, ice, water temperature, and "Dog on the Q. D." to worry me, I did begin to wonder.

For one thing, the *Bear* had no traveling court on board to lay out justice as in the old days. We would capture no sealers, would bring no smuggling vessels to, with a shot across their bows. (I secretly envied the crew of the cutter *Rush* which captured the notorious *Timandra* off St. Michael with its load of illegal liquor for the natives and miners. That must have brought satisfaction! And there was the schooner *Eliza,* also a smuggler, which stranded on St. Lawrence Island under mysterious circumstances.)

We on the *Bear* would not be looking for the old-time whaling ships gripped in the ice. These were things of the past. But surely there must be some important reason for breaking through the ice and facing bleak weather with hazardous ice floes.

I thought about the orders which had been issued long ago to Commodore Wilkins when he first sailed along the shores of the Oregon Territory. They had enjoined him to lend comfort and moral support to the early pioneers by his presence on the frontier, to carry information to and from the settlers, to assure them of governmental interest by the presence of his vessels. But that could hardly be our mission, for we were not making a first trip into a strange land. Ours was merely a repetition of what had been done many times before.

What then? Ubiquity . . . awareness . . . government in being . . . prestige? Perhaps so, for we did carry a few Eskimos, a government school teacher, and a few traders. One of the officers on board was deputized a U. S. Commissioner with authority to carry out whatever duties might arise. The *Bear's* duties were indeed varied.

Under way again, the *Bear* now proceeded to St. Michael. We were many days out of Unalaska, and the ship had worked hard to get us here. One look at that desolate shore told us a man would have to be crazy to want to go to St. Michael.

"Crazy?" said John Lidmann. "Let me tell you about the crazy Finn, who came up here all alone, one man in a boat."

People in the North are apt to be different, and this may mean merely odd, or sometimes extraordinary, or once in a while "crazy." Perhaps they come North because this difference is in their make-up, or perhaps after they come north the land does strange things to them. Whether the "Finn" was unusual when he came North, or turned that way later, no one knows. Old-timers first heard of him in 1905 when a newspaper in Astoria, Oregon, reported he had sailed down from Alaska to the States in an open dory, on a one-man trip a month long. That alone qualified the Finn as

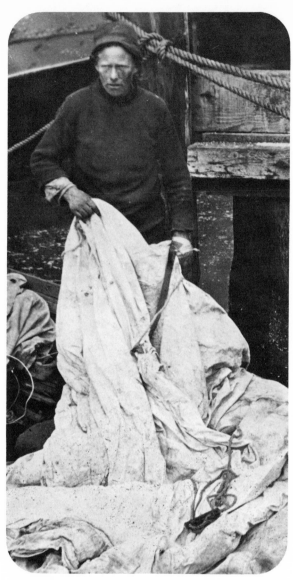

John Pahikkalia was called the "crazy" Finn.

extraordinary, if not crazy. John Pahikkalia was his name, but he was known as the Finn, and, sometimes, the crazy Finn. Next he turned up in Dutch Harbor, to report the codfish schooner *Nellie Coleman* wrecked down around Unga. The Finn hadn't seen the wreck, but he had seen a Frenchman who had, and who said all hands were lost, including the Captain's wife. The Frenchman, so said the Finn, was wearing the Captain's wife's clothes. This seemed to be a little out of the ordinary, also.

Sometime after the war ended in 1918, John Pahikkalia came down to Unalaska from Nome, and John brought with him an old boat engine. At Unalaska he put the engine in a battered old dory, and lived in the boat, wrapped up in an old sail at night for protection against the weather. When winter came, the Finn sank his boat to keep the storms from wrecking it, and when spring came he floated it again, cleaned up the engine, and went fishing. The last anyone heard of the Finn for a time then was that he had gone to St. Michael . . . all that way in an open boat? The Finn *must* be crazy.

A long time later, the Coast Guard Cutter *Haida* was sent up to St. Michael with orders to bring back a crazy man. Two men came aboard. The first one was a mild sort who climbed up the ladder and said, "Well, we're ready to go." After him came a strange being with seabags full of odds and ends, and a hundred yards of salmon gill netting. While the crew wondered what to do with him, he announced he would sleep under a boat with his gear.

"But maybe we ought to lock you up."

"Lock me up! Lock him up—he's the crazy one. I'm the guard, John Pahikkalia."

And so he was. The *Haida* crew never was certain exactly what happened, but they knew one thing, John Pahikkalia got a ride down to Dutch Harbor, and the government paid him for it. Maybe that crazy Finn wasn't so crazy after all.

The *Bear* tugged impatiently at her anchor off St. Michael where we put ashore sacks of mail for people who had not heard from the outside world all winter long. In Golovnin Bay, we lowered our boats to take fresh water out of the snow rivers emptying

We lowered a boat in Golovnin Bay.

into the sea and, as usual, one of our passengers, Mr. Watkins, a strange little man from the Hydrographic Office in Washington, D. C., went ashore to make his scientific observations. Carrying his precious box of instruments, a head full of figures, and his pup tent, he cheerfully went about his business. Once ashore, Mr. Watkins erected his tent on a flat stretch of ground and then disappeared inside with his instruments. We saw little of him until he was ready to quit.

Finally he emerged, stretched himself as would a bear coming out of hibernation and, since the day was cold, flapped his arms like a young seal. Now he adjusted his rimless spectacles on his thin nose, pursed his lips, and silently asked the gray sky if he had forgotten anything. No. Good. He methodically dismantled his gear, folded his tent, and headed back for the ship.

On board, I asked how his trip was.

"Very satisfactory," he answered, taking his little book out of his pocket and recording the data he had gathered.

None of us understood what Mr. Watkins did when he went ashore, but we respected him. He was a good shipmate.

With such an odd assortment of duties and a shipload of such varied personalities, the northerly trip could never be boring. There was an unmistakable thrill in sailing where death lurked for the unwary and unlucky, and those of us who followed the deeds of our predecessors never forgot that what had happened once might happen again—to us.

Sailing the ship close to shore was a constant hazard. The charts showed dangers: muddy bottom, rocks and shoals shrinking to ten, eight, six, and five fathoms. After such a sounding, we quickly steered offshore.

Sometimes it was necessary to run too close for safety in order to get by grounded ice. Often, thick weather made navigation doubly hazardous. At such times, a leadsman was stationed in the chains to take soundings till deep water showed again. The lead was an invaluable aid to the navigator in shallow water, particularly in thick or foggy weather. We used it even when out of sight of land.

Two leads were used for soundings: the hand lead, weighing fourteen pounds, with a line marked to twenty-five fathoms; and the deep-sea lead, weighing fifty pounds, the line being one hundred fathoms in length. Hand soundings sometimes went on for hours, even days, and while hand soundings continued, machine soundings were taken every half hour, sometimes every fifteen minutes. In thick weather, the foghorn boomed continuously, even though we knew there was not a ship within miles. This gave rise to the oft-repeated adage that navigation along the Arctic shores consisted largely of *log line, lead line, and foghorn.* This nobody liked, but there was nothing we could do about it. If the men could not avoid it, they could joke about it, which in any shipload of men is a good sign. They even resorted to pranks to break the monotony.

Tiny was such a prankster. An oversized boy of eighteen, he had not been aboard ship a day before everybody knew him as Tiny. He weighed 225 pounds.

"Your turn in the chains, Tiny," I called to him.

"I shoulda never left home," he said, as he popped the last of a hard biscuit into his mouth.

I knew he was kidding. Tiny loved the *Bear,* but he also loved to gripe. He had a mischievous look on his face, and I wondered what was going on in his mind as he hauled his big body into the chains.

He swung the fourteen-pound lead back and forth in his right hand, squinting ahead into the mist which settled on the rigging in what was nearly ice. The blast of the *Bear's* foghorn was smothered in the thick fog almost before it reached the jibboom. With a long swing, Tiny started the lead over his head in a sweeping circle until it leaped forward and plunged into the sea.

"No bottom at ten!" he called. Time after time he sent the lead leaping into the sea, while the foghorn blasted through the fog above him. This was tiring, cold, monotonous work, and it could go on hour after hour, all night. It had to go on, for there was no other way for Captain Cochran to navigate the *Bear* through the Arctic in fog, or when in shoaling waters.

Now I saw Tiny take an extra swing, putting every ounce of muscle into the heave. The lead soared like a bird, out over the foreyard, to wrap itself around the furled sail.

"No bottom!" he sang out innocently. And then to me, "Watch, I'll put it over the jibboom this time."

Had Tiny lost his mind? I glanced with alarm toward the watch officer, bent over his chart. He hadn't seen the prank. Ought I to warn him that Tiny, bored by monotony, was being a bit foolish? Tiny took another swing and a long heave, and the lead sailed forward, fouled in the backstays and clattered down into the sea. I heard Tiny's laughter suddenly choke into silence. The Captain was on deck! Captain Cochran always had that effect; you knew he was there, even though you couldn't see him.

Instantly all seriousness, Tiny returned to the steady heaving of the lead. "No bottom at ten . . . no bottom at twelve . . . no bottom at ten . . . and a half, nine . . . by the deep eight!" The Captain had reached the bridge and heard the last depth. "Haul her off, Mr. Todd. There's a shoal makes out there just ahead."

"Aye, aye, Sir!"

The *Bear* shifted course off shore into the breeze. Tiny had had his fun. He had found "no bottom" with the lead around the foreyard, but he had most certainly not made a fool of the Captain. And the Captain was making good on his part; he was making a seaman of Tiny.

U p anchor!"

"Steam on the engines!" The black gang sweated below as the *Bear* headed westward across Norton Sound towards a landfall on the southeast end of St. Lawrence Island. It was another gray, bleak day. I glanced sympathetically at Thor as he stood at the edge of the poop deck, staring into the white space. He whined, then began racing around the deck as if obsessed by demons. Finally, panting with exhaustion and futility, he stopped and stared some more.

"We'll send him ashore on the next stop, I should think," said Lieutenant Todd. Clement Todd was an old friend of mine from high school days at Wheat Ridge, Colorado. He had been the duty officer that rainy day when I first boarded the *Bear* at Unalaska, and we paired off on watch for the rest of the trip. "Did you ever have a dog?"

"Sure," I answered. "A big German shepherd. . . ." And so Todd and I were off on another bull session, something to break the monotony of long watches on a cold, gray sea. We covered just about every subject as we reminisced. "Say, remember the time you climbed to the top of the school flagpole, tore down the colors of the rival class, and fastened your own colors to the peak?"

"Do I?" Todd laughed out loud. "And did I ever catch it when I got home that night." He lit his pipe, then leaned on the railing and mused about it. "Yep, Wheat Ridge was quite a place back in 1902. It used to be called Denver's strawberry patch because of all the truck farmers and strawberry pickers. Those farmer boys rode horseback to school sometimes as far as ten miles over snowbound roads."

"We had a lot of chickens," I remembered. "And we had to drive off thieves with shotguns."

Todd glanced up at the swaying mast, the sails now filled with a fair wind. "Remember how farmers buried their winter apples in straw-heaped trenches underground? Boy, I can just taste those juicy apples. That's one thing I miss up here."

I was suddenly curious about the years between high school and now. "What ever made you go to sea?" I asked.

Todd shrugged. "Restlessness, I suppose. I started out by joining the Colorado National Guard to help put down a strike among the miners around Leadville and Cripple Creek. From there I joined the Revenue Cutter Service and came North." He tapped his pipe on the railing and watched the black ashes float out on the wind. "I tried to get out, settle down, but it didn't work. Back I came to serve during the war. . . ."

"And now?"

"Now, I tell you, Alaska is the answer. I want to go

31

into mining. Gold, coal, oil, or whatever it has to offer. The resources are so rich, so untapped. . . ." He broke off, somewhat embarrassed at his display of landlubber talk. "Anyway, I'm going to make a fortune here some day. You wait and see."

At St. Lawrence Island, the cabin boy took Thor ashore to sniff around and run a bit. Paddy, the commissary steward, went ashore to shoot some reindeer. Soon we heard gunfire booming through the eerie quiet. "Paddy is a good shot. We'll eat fresh reindeer steak tonight," Captain Cochran said.

We were standing on the bridge and now the Captain pointed along the island shore. "About there, the old *Corwin* found the wrecked smuggler *Eliza;* took spars and fittings from her to make a jury rudder for herself. Her own rudder had been cracked off in heavy ice." He pointed the other way. "Along there, the *Timandra,* with a load of whiskey and guns for the natives, was stranded. The masts, I believe, were taken by the *Corwin.* Her jibboom had been carried away." He narrowed his eyes as if mentally tying in these memories with his present problems. "A ship has to be self-sustaining, or it had better stay out of the ice."

Paddy and his party returned with seven reindeer carcasses to be used in lieu of beef. The gang triced them up on the forestay, the only cold storage place available, and covered them with canvas to keep the flies and gulls away. The crew would have reindeer meat off and on, for the rest of the season.

"It'll give the men dysentery," Crandall observed sourly.

"They'll get used to it," said Lidmann.

It didn't, exactly, and we did, to some extent.

The *Bear* next sailed north to the lonely mist-shrouded rock known as King Island. Standing just thirty miles off the Alaskan coast, this dreary island, discovered and named by Captain Cook, is only three miles in circumference but was the home of 150 of the hardiest, seagoing Eskimos in Alaska. We anchored in eighteen fathoms off the village, so close to the rocks ashore that we could almost reach out and

touch them. There was no beach nor shelter, but the *Bear,* true to her name as the "Visiting Angel," had urgent business. The natives, in spite of their hardiness, had had a hard winter and our doctor was badly needed. He was soon ashore, pulling teeth, doling out pills, and performing necessary operations.

The entire village nestled against the slope on one side, and the houses were supported on the downhill side by poles, or stilts. Some natives lived in dugouts underground. The sea was too rough for boating that day, and I could see their skin boats, forty-foot *umiaks* and single- or double-seated *kayaks,* placed high on the rocks, out of reach of the ravenous Eskimo dogs.

"I wonder why anybody would voluntarily live in such a dismal, lonely place," I said to John Lidmann. Nothing edible grew on the island except a shrub which the Eskimos chewed as a tonic. There were dogs, as in all Eskimo villages, and sea fowl. But they were the only animal life.

"To make a living, of course." Lidmann then went on to explain that vast herds of walrus came into the Bering Sea from the Arctic Ocean. "Here, right at their front door for the taking, are meat for food, blubber for making oil with which to keep warm, and ivory for making implements, for adornment, and for carving to sell. They also have skins for making boats."

I knew that the King Islanders sold their ivory in Nome, ninety miles away. Every year, about the Fourth of July, every last man, woman, and child, along with dogs and their complete household gear, would abandon the Island and descend on Nome. When they finished piling in all hands on top of their household gear, summer stores, and sealskins full of oil, the boats had about two inches of freeboard left. Choosing a good day, they then made a dash for the mainland about thirty miles away and hugged the coastline all the way to Nome.

After spending their summer in Nome, with twenty-four hours a day of daylight in which to barter and lay in stores, they must then figure out how to get back to the Island. Crammed to the gunwales on the way over, the load for going home was multiplied many times over. Here is where the Coast Guard, usually the *Bear,* came to the rescue. That would be our job. We would see all these people again in Nome.

The natives' houses clung to the steep sides of King Island.

With our immediate job finished at King Island, we then stood away to the southwest along the north shore of St. Lawrence Island. The island, nearly a hundred miles long, was a barren, ice-covered area with high hills hidden by fog. Again, Captain Cochran pointed out each headland with the intimacy of long acquaintance, and the tales eased the monotony of the long watches.

And in the berth deck we talked about the skipper, the man we all knew, but a man about whom we knew very little. "I heard tell he'd studied medicine in his youth. . . ."

"No, that's not right. I happen to know he entered Annapolis in 1883 and graduated in 1887."

"Well, one thing's for sure. He knows the sea and he knows the ice."

Happy LaRue piped up, "If the old Bull Walrus thinks he's going to make a sailor out of me, he's wrong. He never will because I'm a hobo, pure and simple."

Yes, Happy was a hobo, but he was a good shipmate, too. He kept us laughing with the tall tales of the mischief he'd gotten into while riding the rails.

The *Bear* arrived off Gambell at midnight. Though eight bells had been struck, the misty daylight still sheathed the sky. The weather had come to a dead calm. The ice had cleared from in front of the village and even the ocean swell was missing. Mist came down from the hills and clung to the edge of the land.

Steaming into what had been the hazy setting of the sun, we could see a boat outlined to landward. Slowly it grew larger until boat and ship converged. The stranger proved to be a large umiak, deeply loaded with people. At 1:30 a.m., there was still light as the *Bear* dropped anchor.

"Ahoy there. Come aboard," the skipper called.

Immediately the umiak hooked onto the shroud channels and swarms of Eskimos crawled up over the side and swung onto the deck. Arms laden with trade goods, they chattered gaily with the crew. There were sacks of ivory, furs, and trinkets, but first they would show their wares to the Captain's Japanese steward. Like all voyagers to the North, Captain Cochran was not immune to bartering for souvenirs.

On King Island, a woman was boiling walrus blubber.

Everyone who came on board the *Bear* seemed to know him from the past. Squawmen, traders, and natives were all anxious to squat for a spell on the poop deck before mingling with the rest of the ship's company for their trading. I could not help but notice how the natives uttered the Captain's name with a kind of reverence, and he in turn had a great deal of patience with them and their particular wants.

In all the happy confusion of trading at 1:30 in the morning, I noticed a parka-clad man dashing up and down the deck trying to shake hands with anybody who would listen to him. "Hey, there," he grabbed my arm. I whirled around to find myself face to face with a bearded white man. He was so glad to see me he could barely babble his name, Bishop.

"What are you doing here?" I asked.

"I've been stranded all winter," he exclaimed. "You can't know how glad I am to see you."

"But how. . .?"

"Two other men and myself were prospecting for gold last autumn. We were on the mainland above Nome near Teller. As we headed alongshore back toward Nome in our small boat, we were blown out to sea and finally drifted across to St. Lawrence Island."

"How about the others?" I asked, wondering if there were still a chance of rescuing them.

The old sourdough shrugged disinterestedly. "Who knows? They couldn't stand the natives. But me, I was so glad to be on dry land I didn't care. They're probably following the wind to Siberia."

By now I realized the old man didn't want to be rescued. He was perfectly happy to stay on and live with the Eskimos. All he really wanted was someone to hear him out. Was this yet another duty of the *Bear*?

"I was a friend of Jack London's," he said proudly. Now he hauled out a tattered letter he said he had received from California the year before, in which the writer said she remembered "Jack" telling her about him (Bishop) many times . . . about when the two men had hunted gold together in the Klondike. The grimy fish-and-blubber smelling letter was signed, "Charmian London."

Well, thought I, the letter was not the only thing that smelled fishy. That story was a wild one, but in the North, you never know. I winked in amusement at Happy LaRue, who was trading an old shirt for a polar bear skull. Something was brewing in that mischievous mind of his. Soon it happened.

Happy attached a rope to the bear's skull and began dragging it around deck. "The poor bear starved to death," he moaned loudly and dramatically, "just as the men of the *Bear* are going to starve for want of proper food."

"Somebody should throw him a towel to dry those crocodile tears," Lidmann chuckled.

The Eskimos aboard were not sure what the joke was but they laughed just the same. Captain Cochran, pacing back and forth on the quarterdeck above, frowned his disapproval of such antics. "Has it gotten so bad this soon?"

But Happy wasn't finished. He and the other firemen, who had shaved the tops of their heads, formed a line, single file, and began parading around the well deck in full view of the Skipper. Happy winked right and left as the "chain-gang" dramatized their sad lot.

Finally the Captain growled with resignation, "Let 'em get it out of their systems," and turned away.

Ralston, the Master-at-Arms, didn't see the humor or the necessity of such nonsense. With a booming voice he bellowed, "There's gonna be discipline on board here, or else!"

The firemen took one look at the powerful Ralston, then scattered forward.

The excitement was over for awhile. The Eskimos returned ashore, and we busied ourselves stowing away our treasures. Mr. Watkins took notes on the tests he'd made that day while Thor curled up on deck to rest. Later in the day, the doctor, who had been ashore since breakfast, giving pills, pulling teeth, and operating, returned on board. We heard the order, "Up anchor! We're getting under way!"

The *Bear* stood to the westward across the Bering Sea. Ahead lay Siberia.

Captain Cochran bent over his charts, his tan and white reindeer coat covering him to his knees, his cigar clenched tightly in his teeth. He scowled, the leathery skin bunching at his brows. "Have you checked for water temperature?"

"Aye, Sir," I told him. "We seem to be making good time."

"Very well." He seemed to relax now, as much as an iceman could in such waters. We were rounding the end of St. Lawrence Island, a barren, desolate hump of snow and ice. The sight brought memories flooding over him. "That place was a thriving Eskimo village forty years ago, but the whalers destroyed it."

I was taken aback. "You mean the whalers massacred helpless people, Sir? I had always thought they were on friendly terms."

The Captain shook his head. "They didn't kill with guns but with whiskey which they'd traded for ivory and furs. When the Eskimos sobered up, winter was upon them and they could not hunt for food. The *Corwin* found the two hundred bodies. . . ."

We stared at the bleak sight in silence. Finally Captain Cochran blew his nose and finished the last of his mug of coffee. "Ever hear the name of William Reynolds?"

I gulped. "Yes, Sir! He was a Commandant of the Coast Guard."

The Captain smiled and turned away. "It seems a strange coincidence that our Commandant, then a young third lieutenant, was one of the party which landed to discover the tragedy. Forty years later, this same man issued my orders to make this voyage on the *Bear* in the same waters. . . ."

On through the pale night the *Bear* steamed with her sails furled. There wasn't a breath of wind in this narrow strip of sea. It was hard to believe that the Asian mainland was only forty miles away. All the whaleships that ever went into the Arctic passed through this strip as they followed the whale herds moving northward in the summer. The old whalers . . . what tales these waters could tell of them and their lusty battles with the elements and with each other. My favorite story came out of the Civil War.

It was in 1865 that Captain Waddell and the Confederate raider *Shenandoah* swooped down on the Union whaler *Favorite*. "Haul down your flag!" he demanded.

Captain Young of the *Favorite* was cocky and defiant. "Haul it down yourself, damn you, if you think it will be good for your constitution!"

The reply was quick in coming. "If you don't haul it down we will blow you out of the water!"

37

"Blow away, me buck!" thundered Captain Young. "But may I be eternally damned if I haul down that flag for any cursed Confederate pirate that ever floated!" Seizing a pistol, he attempted to shoot the officer from the *Shenandoah* who had been sent on board his ship. But as he squeezed the trigger, there was only a dull, harmless "click." "What be this?" he shouted. "My own cowardly officers have unloaded my pistol!"

"Resistance would have been useless," they told him sadly. "A whaler would stand no chance against a man-of-war."

The flag came down. The *Favorite,* fired by the boarding party, burst into flames. Captain Young, watching from his prison aboard the *Shenandoah,* saw his own ship flounder and sink, but all the while cursed the freebooter who had brought him to such a sorry pass.

The *Bear,* approaching the Siberian shore now, ran into flat ice which got thicker, then showed many heavy hummocks. The heavy ice brought forth another of those classic tales of sea disaster such as the whalers lived through and sometimes died for in their hard life searching for blubber.

"I wonder what ever happened to the whalers *Vigilant* and *Mt. Wallaston,*" I mused aloud, subconsciously identifying myself with those early seafarers as we sailed "their" waters. "And Captain Ebeneezer Nye, skipper of the *Mt. Wallaston;* he was quite a man, wasn't he?"

"Aye, he was that, all right." John Lidmann leaned on the rail to watch the ice cakes. "He tangled with the *Shenandoah* during the Civil War when he was aboard the whaler *Abigail* out of New Bedford. He managed to get away with some of his crew in a small boat."

"I heard they traveled by boat and on foot along the edge of the ice for a hundred miles to warn other whalers," I said, remembering accounts I had read. "It was in 1879 that Nye, commanding the *Mt. Wallaston,* sailed north in search of whales and was joined by the *Vigilant.* Both took whales, and steered into the ice for more . . . right where we are now."

Lidmann lit his pipe, and now the glowing embers gave a warm light in the mist. "The whaler *Helen Mar* was supposed to have spoken with the two ships while they were taking whales, then lost them in the fog and ice. They disappeared off Herald Island near Point Hope, far to the North." He shook his head, but didn't turn. I knew that he too felt a kinship with the lost whalers. "Eskimos along the Siberian shore found the hull of a ship resembling the *Vigilant,* battered and dismasted, with four dead bodies lying in their bunks. The natives took what gear they could carry and left the ship to be crushed and sunk by the ice."

"Did they find anything that could be identified?" I wondered.

"Strangely enough, a pair of spectacles known to have belonged to Captain Nye," Lidmann said. "And you know, there's a funny thing, too. The *Corwin* has a book called *McClure's Discovery of the Northwest Passage,* which says that walrus do not eat fish or seal. Well, in the margin of this book is a notation, 'They eat both fish and seal. . . .' signed, 'E. F. Nye.' And the signature is genuine."

"What a man Nye must have been," I observed. "To the end, he was still taking issue with somebody, as he had with the raider." Hearing footsteps behind me, I snapped to from my musings on the assumption that it could always be the Captain. It wasn't.

"Hey, Happy, why so sad?" Lidmann chuckled at LaRue's downcast mood.

"I'm cold. I want to go back to being a hobo in the deep, deep South," he said.

"We were talking about the whalers *Vigilant* and *Mt. Wallaston,*" I said. "Ever hear of them?"

"I guess so," he said with feigned boredom. "Everybody knows everybody else's business in Alaska, even ancient history."

Lidmann went back to our story of the incident. "Searchers for the lost *Mt. Wallaston, Vigilant,* and the explorer ship *Jeannette* sailed to a position of 70 degrees North latitude and 176 degrees West longitude and came back south to search the beaches in Emma Harbor, Providence Bay, on around to Whalen at East Cape. Quite a feat, I'd say."

"Hey," said Happy, his eyes widening with the realization that he was literally at the spot where so many shipwrecks had occurred. "You don't suppose history will repeat itself. . . ."

Emma Harbor was filled with solid, flat ice . . . .

Lidmann and I both laughed. "Remember, we're the rescuers. We don't dare wreck ourselves," Lidmann pointed out. "Besides, as a matter of record, the present Commandant of the Coast Guard was one of the young men sent ashore in Siberia to hunt for traces of the *Vigilant,* the *Mt. Wallaston* and the De Long Expedition's *Jeannette.*"

"And," I remembered, "he's the same person who just sent a wireless dispatch to Captain Cochran directing the *Bear* to assist the *Maud,* stranded in the same waters."

"Ain't that somethin'?" chortled Happy. "Roundy-come-roundy."

By daylight the next day we raised the white peaks of the Asian continent looming above the streak of mist which was the horizon. We ran into Providence Bay, then into a landlocked bight known as Emma Harbor. It was filled with solid, flat ice. Looking around us as we crunched our way in, we could see mountains on three sides, rising steeply out of the ice-covered water. Barren, half snow-clad, they appeared as silent, prehistoric monsters and, for a little while, a hushed awe settled over the *Bear.* Even Happy was taken aback at the gigantic splendor of the scene. At last he said, "Now ain't *that* something, Ransom? You better put that in the book."

"I will," I said. "I'll make notes, but I'm going to use my camera, too."

"You know," said Happy, "I'm glad we had to come here to clean our boilers and take on fresh water before going on to help the *Maud.* It'll give us a chance to see some real Siberian natives. What are they called?"

"Chukchis."

Happy leaned over the rail to wave to them as they came along the coast in their boats. Soon, they fell in behind and followed us all the way down the channel. We circled the harbor, slicing the ice to bits, then came to anchor.

Immediately, several of the boats came alongside and their people clambered aboard. Noisy, happy, and chattering in their native tongue, they intrigued us by their odd appearance. The women and little girls had covered their faces with tattoo marks and parted

The Innuits combined American dress with Eskimo parkas.

40

their thick black hair in the middle to braid it down the back. Happy was the first one to mingle with them as they danced around with a shuffling, swinging motion. He seized one of the women and began waltzing around the deck with her. "They know how to dance," he said gleefully. "Put that down in your book."

The men and boys cut their hair crown-free, with a ring of long hair around the sides of the head and over the ears, allowing the long loose hair to hang down their backs. We thought it odd that their faces were not tattooed, as were the women's. One old man who seemed to be the interpreter shook hands with Captain Cochran.

"We very glad to see American revenue cutter come here. We get chewing tobacco now. All winter we have none. We very glad."

We gave each native man a cigarette. When the women refused, the interpreter explained, "Very bad for women to smoke, but she chew if you give her chewing tobacco."

American money was no good to them as a means of exchange so we settled by giving them food and tobacco. I could not help but note, unkindly, that the Siberians were far more filthy than the American natives, the Innuits, that we had been used to. And that was going some!

In addition to taking on fresh water, cleaning our boilers, and checking on the medical needs of the natives, we had yet another reason for stopping at Emma Harbor. Three of our passengers who were miners were dead set on going ashore to hunt for gold in the Siberian mountains. "We'll have to have our supplies put ashore," they said. So Berg, the boatswain, had his gang break their gear out of the hold—enough to sustain them for months—load it into a boat, and land it on shore. One of the party sat on the supplies on the beach to keep the natives from stealing them, while the leader headed for the Russian agent's log house to get permission to prospect.

"This looks like a good time to go ashore to take pictures," I said to Mr. Weaver, the carpenter. "Want to come along?"

"Sure," he said. "I'm as curious as the next man."

The Russian agent lived in the only log house in the village, which stood at the mouth of a rushing stream coming out of the nearby mountains. Stretched

The Chukchis were dirty, but happy.

out for half a mile on either side of the agent's house were fifteen or twenty native houses. The land itself was a morass of tundra, through which seeped the snow water. Wading through this for half a mile, we finally spotted a particularly picturesque Siberian house. "You call it a *yaranga,*" I said, aiming my camera.

It was round, about twenty feet in diameter and ten feet high at the center, through which the ends of driftwood braces stuck out, as in the frame of an American Indian wigwam. The covering of this yaranga was walrus skins although other houses had used bits of canvas, no doubt from sails of wrecked ships. I noticed, too, that whale ribs were used as braces when driftwood was not available. Some of the natives had built yarangas of sod for use in winter, and lived in the lighter ones only in summer.

"I suppose we ought to see the owner of the house," I said. "Maybe we can get inside if we play our cards right."

We found a native woman in parka, skin pants, and mukluks squatting outside the door before a fire built of driftwood. She was cooking bits of walrus meat in a black pot over the fire. The hood of her parka was thrown off and the loose fit of the garment exposed her back to the waistline. It was filthy. She returned our smiles with a toothless grin, then motioned to her two small boys who were crouched in the doorway peeking out.

"May we take your picture?"

She did not understand. "How do you say it in Siberian?" I asked Weaver. We had come this far for our pictures and I was determined to win out over this language barrier.

Weaver reached into his pocket. "Like this." He pulled out a cigarette, put it in her mouth, and lit it. She sputtered and puffed away. Finally she nodded her head in consent and gestured with her hands, still greasy from cutting the walrus meat, that she was perfectly willing to pose.

After I snapped the shutter, she said, "Gum."

"Sure." Weaver winked as he produced a stick for her and one for each of the boys. Our language problems were solved. We would have the grand tour after all.

One small door led into the house. In the back

center was an inner, or second, room which was used for sleeping only. I later learned that at bedtime the entire family stripped naked, just as they did on the American side, then covered themselves with reindeer hide for warmth. The floor itself was covered with skins. In the morning, the sides of the inner house could be rolled up in order to give more daytime living room. Heating in winter was provided by oil lamps. Also, in winter the cooking fire was built on the inside of the outer house. The smoke on the ceiling of this particular yaranga indicated much usage over many winters.

We weren't inside long before we could smell all of them—fish, blubber, unwashed bodies, and filth had all left their fragrant marks, convincing us that outside was better by far.

We wandered back across the bog, visiting every hut in the village and finding dirt, filth, smells, kids, dogs, and weather-worn men and women in all of them. But time was wearing on. We would have to cut short our sight-seeing and head back for the *Bear.*

There were several problems involved in getting back. One was that we had no boat to get to the *Bear* which lay a mile out in the harbor.

"There's a native in an umiak. Let's hail him," Weaver said, as he waved his arms. The fare was a piece of chewing tobacco for the old man and a stick of chewing gum for each of the daughters. They paddled, he steered, and we marveled at their skill.

"What in the world are those?" I asked, pointing to a sealskin blown full of air and tied at both ends. They looked like car fenders to me.

"Um," grunted the man. "We catch 'em walrus. Throw in water with line. Walrus strike at seal. We throw spear. Him dead. Very good!"

Weaver nudged me. "He means they use it as a decoy."

"I see."

"Um," agreed the native, urging his daughters to pull faster. But I am sure he did not know what we were talking about.

Back on board the *Bear,* we soon learned that in spite of hours of dickering and pleading with the Russian agent, the three miners had been refused permission to prospect. "And now," said Berg the boat-swain, "we've got to put all this stuff back in the hold! Civilians! O.K., men, turn to!"

As we made ready to leave Emma Harbor, I reviewed the events of the day and especially my contacts with the natives at this remote spot. Again, there was that queer feeling of kinship, for had not these same people, or their fathers, watched the whaleships pass and seen them wrecked? Had they not gone out on the ice to find the broken hulls and dead bodies of, for instance, the *Vigilant* and the *Mt. Wallaston?* The village was even now reminiscent of that era; the ruin of an old New Bedford whaleboat still lay on the beach, and the bits of canvas wrapped around the roofs of the yarangas could certainly have come from a square sail of one of those unfortunate whalers.

43

The *Bear* hauled around East Cape on July 10 and stood in for anchorage. As the anchor went down with a splash, the wind began to blow strongly from the northwest. The village of Whalen, which was no more than a group of shacks covered with snow, lay in the bight. Between us and the village, the white-hulled *Maud,* which we had come to assist, rode at anchor. Near her lay the *Herman*. Beyond them, along the northern horizon, the iceblink indicated heavy ice, but the water around us was clear.

For two days the stormy winds continued to howl and blow with icy cold, and we would not dream of lowering a boat unless there were vital work to be done. We were white men, and in this element, we dared not take foolish and unnecessary chances. But the Chukchis paid no attention to the weather. In the thick of the storm, a boatload of them came on board to trade.

"They must be crazy," I observed, as they wallowed in the heavy gale. "Or else darned curious."

"Um," said Happy, the linguist.

On second thought, I realized that these natives simply had to investigate each strange ship that came to their land. In former days, there had been the whalers, but now it could be anything from a trader to an explorer ship to a cutter. A trader, of course, meant a sale for their ivory, walrus hides, feather parkas, and other hand-made souvenirs. In exchange, they would receive precious flour, molasses, or sugar, which would be made into "sourdough," a basic food good for quick warmth and energy.

As usual, wherever the *Bear* stopped, the old-timers knew her for what she was—their visiting angel— their light from the mysterious outside world. We watched their antics now, which had almost become a routine, as they climbed aboard, jabbered, grinned, and squatted around amidst their wares, which they spread out on deck. Captain Cochran had allowed them the use of the upper deck, and we were about to settle down to our usual business of trading when a man leaped out from among them. A surprise? Yes and no. For we had come to regard the "odd" situation as the norm.

Filthy, begrimed, unshaven, he introduced himself as Julius Silverman, a trader. "You have got to help us," he said in almost breathless haste. "Our trading schooner was driven ashore by a gale down the coast behind East Cape!"

"But how did you get here?" It was the Captain who strode into our midst. He had one eyebrow cocked as if he were skeptical of this man. Had we not met up with the same kind of story in Gambell when the bewhiskered prospector Bishop poured out his tale of woe? Unlike Bishop, however, Silverman seemed anxious for rescue.

Silverman, the trader, asked for our aid at East Cape.

"I walked around the mountains," the man said. "It was a long way over the boggy tundra but I knew I had to find the *Bear*. My two partners are waiting for help. Will you send a boat for them?"

Captain Cochran scowled. "Impossible."

"But . . . they cannot be abandoned!" Silverman pleaded.

The skipper went on, "We are standing by the *Maud* and, when the weather permits, we will take her in tow. The *Bear* cannot take on more responsibility than she is capable of maintaining."

"Well, then," persisted Silverman, who by now was nearly beside himself with anxiety, "would the *Bear* lay-to off the place where we were shipwrecked? I could send an Eskimo as a messenger to tell them to be ready to come off in a boat."

We waited tensely for the skipper's reply. It would be inhuman to abandon those men, and, after all, was this not our task, to save lives?

"That is also impossible," the Captain gestured helplessly, now softening his harsh tone. "The *Bear* would be too far out to sea." What then? We all forgot the chattering natives as we visualized the fate of those marooned men. Something had to be done.

Captain Cochran turned away, gripped the railing, and said, "Have your men on board the *Bear* by sailing time. That is all I can do for you." He left us with the problem, for there were other urgent matters requiring his attention.

"I guess you'll have to go back after them," I said, sympathetically.

Silverman took a deep breath and stared out over the whiteness. The storm was still bad. He had risked his life to get here, now he must walk twenty miles back around the mountains to get his partners. Anything could happen . . . including the most heartbreaking of all: not returning in time to catch the *Bear*. "I'll leave at once," he said.

I clapped him on the shoulder and shook his hand. "Good luck." What else could one say?

As he went ashore in the umiak, Happy said, "Wonder if those fellows know what kind of a friend they've got."

"If . . . when they get back, I'll be sure to tell them," I vowed.

46

The whistle signal was given. The whaleboat with the running line rowed over to the stricken *Maud.* Next came the towline. Mr. Fedderson went with the boat and made the towline fast around the *Maud's* foremast. The wind veered to the northeast, threatening to drive us shoreward. The *Bear* hove short and by 1:00 p.m. we were ready to start around the misty mountain known as East Cape with the *Maud* in tow.

Every moment was frantic now as we hurried to get under way. Orders flew from the bridge. The crew scurried about their jobs, but there was an unspoken pall which had settled over the ship. Those men—and Silverman—plunging through the white snow and boggy tundra. They were not going to make it after all. We could not possibly slow up our work and delay the ship or we all might be lost.

Suddenly there came a call from the crow's nest. "There they are! Umiak coming alongside!"

Everyone crowded the rail to welcome the exhausted men as they climbed aboard. They were all dressed in sealskin breeches with heavy parkas on top of their other clothes. Encrusted with ice and with snow falling from their mukluks, they somehow managed to grin with pleasure at our reception. Captain Cochran hailed them from the bridge. His face was impassive, but we all knew how he felt. Their welfare had been on his mind constantly after duty had forced him to deny Silverman's request. "About time!" he called. Then, "Stand by on the engines! We're getting under way."

Two days later, we cast the *Maud* adrift off St. Lawrence Island. Silverman and his friends were to sail south on her. With fair wind and sails set, the little explorer ship bore away toward the southern islands and Dutch Harbor. The *Unalga,* my old ship, was en route north to meet her. The *Bear* went on about her duties as if saving a ship, saving lives, was routine to her. Anything was routine to the *Bear.*

Our next port of call was Nome. The *Bear* was unable to take on coal in the open roadstead there because the heavy swells kept her on her beam ends. Our only alternative was to head for St. Michael where we could coal from barges. Unfortunately, coal was the last item in the steamer *Victoria's* hold. We would simply have to wait until she had unloaded her pas-

The Bear *took the stricken* Maud *under tow.*

47

sengers and freight from Seattle and San Francisco. Most of us did not mind the delay for we had realized long ago that a trip aboard the *Bear* would never be a speed run. Slow, but dependable, that was the *Bear*.

While we waited, some of the *Bear's* crew held small arms target practice on the Army range, while the cabin boy took Thor for a romp in the tundra. When the coal had still not been broached, we formed shore parties to wander around town along the waterfront. We were fascinated by the Yukon river steamers, many of which, though built in Dutch Harbor, resembled Mark Twain's Mississippi River steamers. We examined them with practiced eyes as only sailors would. "Notice the bow . . . clumsy to handle in weather . . . wouldn't trust it . . . well, I wouldn't be too sure. . . ." Some of the steamers had been hauled out on the beach; others were stranded in the mud like sick whales, never to move again.

This had been the glory of the Yukon. John Lidmann observed, "It don't look like much now."

"Aye," I said, feeling unreasonably sentimental. "Even the ghosts have left."

We wandered outside the town to examine the two blockhouses which were built by the Russians. Gunports aimed at the water approaches reminded me of stories I had heard about the troubles the Russians had had with the Indians. About that time, a little half-breed girl with long, black, shiny hair wandered up to us. Her eyes sparkled with curiosity as she turned her head from side to side.

"We are from that ship." I pointed to the *Bear*. "You like her?"

The little girl nodded.

"What's your name?"

"Cecilia." Her voice had a curious lilt to it, probably because she was not used to saying her name aloud.

"She might well be a granddaughter of one of the Indians that gave the Russians so much trouble," said Lidmann. "Maybe even Larryown himself. . . ."

"How do you spell 'Cecilia'?" John asked, amused.

She put her hand to her mouth. Her eyes widened. "I . . . I don't know." She turned and ran away.

48

We started back to the ship, each lost in his own thoughts. The story of Larryown had been told and

Cecelia was curious but timid.

retold among icemen as a glaring example of the hatred and tempers of those early days when the Indians were warring between themselves and against the white man. It was in 1850 that the *Enterprise* came into the Bering Sea on a rescue mission. Stopping off at this fort before proceeding to the Arctic, Captain Collinson heard rumors that white men had been seen in the interior, higher up the Yukon Valley. What did it mean? There was only one way of finding out: Send someone to investigate. The man chosen was Lieutenant Barnard who promptly went ashore and followed the river one hundred miles or more up to the village of Nulato. There, he found a full-blown Indian war in progress with rival factions killing one another mercilessly. Before he could send for help, he was stricken with a fever and, as he lay helplessly in bed, an Indian named Larryown stabbed him to death.

Some called it murder, others merely a battle between the natives which resulted in the death of an unfortunate bystander. The curious part of the whole matter was that Larryown was never punished for his crime. In fact, he was considered somewhat of a hero by the local people. Traders continued to curry his favor through the years and by the time the *Corwin* called at Nome in 1880, it was learned that Larryown had just died a peaceful death. Now, in 1921, it was hard to visualize these peaceful, friendly natives as being capable of such a murder. Probably little Cecilia had never even heard the story.

"Coal barge alongside! Cockbill the foreyard! All hands lay out gear!" Old, reliable Hans Berg shouted the orders as the barge loaded with coal from the *Victoria* came alongside.

It was an all-night job, taking the coal aboard, a job that brought grimy sweat running down our backs as the night air whisked cold about us. Hour after hour we tugged, heaved, hauled, and stowed. Even the deck force which had been standing sea watches turned to on the exhausting, though necessary, job.

We could go nowhere without coal.

"July 26," I noted in the ship's log. The clock indicated that it was nearly "morning," an hour which in other parts of the world would mean sunrise. For us there was no change at all, except in time. We would soon be ready to get under way again.

"Cast off the barge!" Captain Cochran ordered. Now came the flurry of umiaks paddling ashore while the *Bear's* boats were brought alongside, hoisted, and secured. "Anchor detail, man your station!"

"Heave 'round on the anchor. Anchor at forty-five fathoms . . . anchor at fifteen fathoms. . . ." And, finally, "Anchor at short stay, anchor in sight, anchor clear!" We were getting under way.

"Engine one-third ahead, left full rudder!" The Captain's voice mingled with the screeching of the birds swooping overhead, with the creaks, groans, and bells of the *Bear*. It was glorious and exhilarating. I supposed it was all a matter of viewpoint since sea terms, sea atmosphere, and sea experiences had always fascinated me. They seldom became boring or routine but continued to be like facets of an exquisitely cut gem. And now, as I stood at the rail watching the waves feather out from our bow and the foam frothing against our hull, I felt an overwhelming surge of gratitude for all this—my life at sea.

"Steady up on course two-seven-zero." Captain Cochran, in heavy boots and reindeer coat, swayed with the ocean's roll. Beside him, tongue hanging out and ears drooping, was Thor, looking wistfully at the disappearing shoreline as heavy gray fog enveloped us. We were headed for Golovnin Bay where we would take on fresh water from the snow rivers before heading for Nome. And at Golovnin Bay, we were at "all hands" again as we lowered our boats with the landing parties.

As usual, Mr. Watkins trundled ashore with his pup tent and instruments. Also in that first boat were the two young men we'd picked up earlier in Nome—Alfred M. Bailey and Russell W. Hendee. As biological specimen hunters, they were out to collect specimens of birds and animal life for the Denver Museum of Natural History. Consequently, each time the *Bear* stopped long enough for a landing party, Bailey and Hendee were the first in the boat, away to hunt and to trade with the natives for odds and ends of the region which they would use in their intended display of northern life. With them, too, was a husky brute of

49

The boats kept busy in Golovnin Bay.

an Airedale dog who thrived on ship life and hunting on the tundra flats, much to the dismay of poor Thor.

Now, after having been placed ashore, they began to hunt, and soon we could hear the reports of their guns echoing across the bogs and ice-encrusted bays. Before long, they rowed back to the *Bear* and climbed aboard ship with triumphant grins and armloads of treasures. This time they had some ivory, a few bones of seals and walrus, and some seabirds. They immediately headed for the well where they skinned their catch, then treated the feathers and hides for packing and later shipment to the outside.

"I don't get it," said Happy, shaking his head. "There they are, buried up to their elbows in blood, gore, and chemicals and yet they're having the time of their lives."

"Does seem strange," I agreed. "But then maybe they think *we're* loco for being sailors. Anyway, you've got to agree they're good-natured and they also provide us with a few laughs now and then."

As we began to take on water, we noticed how the bay gleamed white with broken water. Whitecaps, but they did not run with the wind. I pointed them out to John Lidmann. "They don't act like other whitecaps I've seen."

"They're whales—belugas. And I'd just as soon wait until they leave before getting on with the watering. They get playful, but a whale can play rough."

My skin prickled with excitement as I watched the beasts roll about on the surface, then up flukes in a dive, then burst out of the water to crash back down in a welter of bright spray. They completely ignored the *Bear* and her puny boats. This was their sea—we were the intruders. When I contrasted our eggshell boats to the powerful whales, I didn't mind waiting until they had gone. I was in no hurry.

Water aboard, hunters back, the *Bear* headed across Norton Sound, steaming at night as usual, arriving at Nome at eight in the morning. Now it was "all hands" to take on passengers and freight for Point Barrow. The passengers were government school teachers, sent to replace those who were going "outside"; traders who had been outside and were coming back to their northern homes; and a few Eskimos who sampled the glories of the white man's life as far south as San Francisco and were now returning to the simple life of their forefathers.

Our freight included food, clothing, medicines, and mail. The mail was the last anyone would receive until next year. For entertainment during the long winter at Point Barrow, the school teachers had a piano, which was gingerly hoisted aboard the *Bear*.

All day long the *Bear's* boats shuttled to and from the Nome beach. Near the end of the afternoon watch, the boats were finally hoisted, the gear secured for sea. The men returned to their regular watches, the anchor came up, and the *Bear* stood to the westward.

While the boats had been loading, on the nearby beach we could see the King Islanders who were summering in Nome. As we left Nome, the wind shifted around the compass and the sounds of their singing and chanting came over the water as clearly as if we had been in their very midst. To those of us who were Midwesterners, the Eskimo chants sounded like those of the plains Indians and the howling of the dogs was as melancholy as the wailing of coyotes. Even the throbbing rhythm of their crude drums had a strangely familiar beat.

But soon the wind veered and the sounds died away. Now all we could hear was the age-old music of the sea: the hum of wind in the rigging, the creak of the hull, the splash and rumble of cold gray water against the *Bear's* sturdy sides.

"Quartermaster! Strike eight bells."

"On deck the watch!"

The time was 4:00 p.m., the start of the first dog watch. As I struck the ship's bell, I read again the engraved legend, "T. F. Secor and Co., New York, 1838," and wondered what ship had first carried it. Truly, the *Bear* was a link between the old and the new and I could not calm the surge of pride I felt for her. I would not have traded her for all the modern steamships in the world. I gazed up proudly at the *Bear's* four little square sails on the foremast, the trysail brailed up behind them, the mainsail and mizzen that flapped helplessly when the wind died, and the three skimpy headsails out on the jibboom. For me it was a never-ending source of wonder and joy to see this sky-thrusting spectacle of ropes and sails, masts and spars, dancing before the wind.

At last the *Bear* had begun the long trip to the top of the world. We were on our way North. By this time the crew and passengers had their definite ideas about life aboard the *Bear*. Some few grumbled louder about the food and living conditions, yet surprisingly many of the early gripers had settled into the routine as if they had been born to it.

The *Bear's* crew ate chow in the low-ceilinged berth deck where tables hung down on rope lanyards from the overhead beams. These lanyards helped steady the table when it swung back and forth to the heave of the *Bear,* as she rammed her way through the floes in the semitwilight of the Arctic evening. The only light came from a small skylight and the few electric bulbs. We never forgot that we were at sea, for standing in the middle of the berth deck between the mess tables was the foremast which fitted into the keelson far below. Always, as we ate, there was the creaking and groaning sound of the mast and the grumble and scrape of ice as the *Bear* pushed onward, north to Point Barrow.

Life aboard the *Bear* consisted of long spells of loneliness and isolation, when our small world was cut off completely from other living things. Consequently, when we sighted a ship, we were intensely interested in everything about her. Each vessel was a personality and we speculated on her appearance and behavior as one would on a new neighbor in a small-town community.

"Blimey, there's a beaut if I ever saw one," piped our British fisherlad as he spotted the British auxiliary schooner *Lady Kindersley,* a trader-whaler from Vancouver, British Columbia. She was three-masted, carry-

53

ing trade goods from Vancouver which she would exchange for furs and ivory.

"Who owns her?" I asked.

"Hudson's Bay Company," John Lidmann explained. "She was built to take the place of the *Karluk* which was wrecked off Wrangel Island in 1913. The *Bear* rescued the crew of the *Karluk*." The two ships would meet again three years later. The *Lady Kindersley* would be wrecked at Point Barrow, and the *Bear* would rescue her crew, too.

The *Bear* passed Teller and Point Clarence, headed for Cape Prince of Wales. Captain Cochran, from the detailed chart he kept in his head, pointed out places of interest.

"Right there," he said, "the *Redfield* stranded back in 1911. She hit the shoal and never got off. Fog, of course. Old man McKenna had her."

I moved myself over closer so as not to miss a word of his story.

"The *Redfield* was named after the Yankee skipper of the whaler *Abigail*, the last vessel to be seized and burned by the Confederate raider *Shenandoah*."

"Didn't that really happen after the war ended, Sir?" I asked.

"That's right," he said. "The *Abigail* knew the war was over, but *Shenandoah* wouldn't believe it. The U. S. Navy sent the sloops-of-war *Saranac* and *Suwannee* out scouting for her, but she was never caught."

"What became of the *Saranac* and *Suwannee?*" I questioned.

Captain Cochran pursed his lips in thought. "Yes . . . yes, now I remember. After the United States bought Alaska, they cruised in Alaskan waters to help the development of the territory. In 1868 the *Suwannee* was wrecked off the Queen Charlotte Islands and the *Saranac* rolled over and sank in Seymour Narrows in 1875."

I shuddered. "That was a sad ending for good ships, Sir. Not a very happy fate for them."

"But a usual one for these waters," he pointed out.

The *Bear* was getting closer in now, and Captain Cochran concluded his narrative by nodding towards the shoal making out inside Cape Prince of Wales. "Right there the whaler *Sea Ranger* stranded and

broke up in 1894. She was running in to bury a seaman who had died at sea. The captain wanted to give him a decent burial and got wrecked for his efforts."

Down splashed the *Bear's* anchor and I could not help the feeling of relief that our old ship was safe—at least for the moment.

Soon, the weather cleared so that we could see the gathering of little huts which was called Kingegan, and even King Island came into view to the south. Westward, Big and Little Diomede Islands loomed up, and we could faintly see East Cape on the Siberian shore. Behind us lay the Bering Sea and ahead lay the Arctic Ocean. It was an awesome moment for those of us who had been so used to being "closed in" by weather.

I noted these sights in my diary along with a mention of our itinerary. We would visit Kotzebue Sound and round Cape Lisburne. Then would come Point Hope, Icy Cape, Wainwright, and Point Barrow—all pinpoints on an enormous map of mystery and cold danger. Our final destination was Demarcation Point, the line which separates Alaska from Canada. "How many men," I scribbled, "have traveled such a route? How many men could have fortune smiling on them so sweetly? In this year of 1921, aboard the *Bear,* I have found my destiny. I have become an iceman. . . ." I winced at this sentimental outburst and quickly scratched it out. Instead I noted in a most business-like way that all was well thus far and that we were proceeding on schedule to our designated ports-of-call. It was one thing to talk through your hat while leaning on the rail with a shipmate. It was quite another to leave a permanent record for the eyes of cynics.

Each day I learned something new, as the ship moved farther north.

"Remember my mentioning the *Helen Mar* some time back?" Captain Cochran asked. "Well, it was right here that she ran into trouble back in 1892 as she lay in the ice, cutting up a whale. Nearby, the steam whaler *Jesse H. Freeman* had also harpooned a whale which immediately dove under the ice in a wounded frenzy. The *Freeman* began ramming into the floes, tracing the whale by its blood. About that time, fog set in, and the two vessels were completely hidden from each other."

The Northern Light *had a mutiny during the gold rush.*

"Did the *Freeman* ever get her whales in?"

"Eventually," the Captain said. "But when the fog lifted, the *Helen Mar* had disappeared. The *Freeman* searched and finally found one man on the ice. Forty-eight hours later, the steam whaler *Orca* found four more bruised and exhausted, stranded on the ice. They were the only survivors from the *Helen Mar.*"

"The way I heard it," John Lidmann added, "was that the ship got nipped between two large bergs and crushed before the boats could get clear. The men saved themselves by clinging to the mainmast which had been thrown over the ice. Of the four men picked up by the *Orca,* two died of exposure, which brought the death list to thirty."

As the *Bear* cruised along, we passed over the spot where the whaler *Ohio* was crushed in the ice with the loss of twenty men. We anchored at Kotzebue Sound, where the *Northern Light* had a mutiny of sorts during the gold rush days. The crew wanted to break their shipping articles, but their Captain would not agree. So six men bored holes in the hull near the keel so the ship would sink and thus relieve them of their contract. But the Captain outsmarted them, found the holes, and ordered the water pumped out. The ship was saved.

Icy Cape. Treeless, bleak, white with last winter's snows, and lonely. It was here that Captain Cook, in his last voyage of discovery, had come to anchor as he searched for the Northwest Passage. With him was Captain Bligh. Bligh had ranged up and down Cook Inlet in Alaska and proved that it was not the Northwest Passage. He circled Bristol Bay, and sailed into Dutch Harbor around Cape Cheerful. He commanded a ship of the line under Nelson at the battle of Copenhagen, had become an admiral and, finally, Commandant of the *H. M. Dockyard* at Portsmouth, England.

And yet Captain Bligh, of the Royal Navy, master navigator and hardy iceman in unknown Alaskan waters, was now known for only one thing—the mutiny in the *Bounty.*

55

Off Icy Cape, the greatest whaling ship disaster of all time occurred in 1871. During each winter, the Arctic ice reaches down into the Bering Sea. Each spring this vast field of ice begins to break away at the south, gradually receding northward so that by May or June ships can push through to the Bering Strait and on to the Arctic Ocean.

The whale herd follows this ice field as it recedes, usually under the ice itself. Each year the whaleships trailed the herds up the coast of Japan and entered the Bering Sea, usually from the southwest, stopping finally at the edge of the white barrier. Then the ships would be strung along the edge of the ice for miles, vessel after vessel, as far as the eye could see.

Around the first of May, in 1871, the whalers from the Japan Sea began arriving, crunching through the ice south of Cape Thaddeus on the Siberian shore, a little to the southwest of Bering Strait.

During the first part of June, the wind remained light and variable, but a great deal of fog lay over the ice. In mid-June, the ice had broken up and the whalers stood northward, taking a few more whales on the way. By the time the fleet reached Plover Bay, a small bight on the Siberian coast, the whales had all passed into the Arctic Ocean.

These early whalers were playthings of the ice packs, treacherous currents, and contrary winds.

Knowledge of the ice was a major part of navigation in the whaling region. Whaleship captains learned that the Eskimos could give them better information about what to expect from wind and ice in the North than could charts and the heavens.

That year the Eskimos told the whalemen they would be jammed in if they hugged the American shore too closely. "But that's where most of the whales are," the whalers said. "We'll continue on." Seven of the forty skippers thought better of it, however, and returned south.

The first disaster came on June 14 when the barkentine *Oreole* was stove in by the ice. Such a mishap was not unusual. The other captains, some of whom had wives and families on board, shrugged off the incident and kept on through the ice. By June 30, all the ships had passed the Bering Strait into the Arctic Ocean.

The hunters were given another reminder of the dangers that lay ahead when at East Cape, the survivors of the ship *Japan* came aboard after their long winter's stay ashore among the natives. Their ship had been caught and crushed in the ice the previous October. The crew of thirty-one had begun their long trek for the Siberian shore, but eight of them had perished. The survivors lived among the natives for nine months, subsisting on rotten walrus blubber.

57

Now these men were distributed among the fleet, each of them glad to be aboard ship once more. They were willing to take the chance of being wrecked again, rather than remain as they were.

Most of June and July remained foggy. Late in July, strong winds set in from the northeast, swinging around to the southeast. This cleared the American shore of ice and the fleet stood for Icy Cape. Much ice had grounded there along the shore, but the shallow-draft vessels crept in behind it. The wind moderated on August 6 and the ice began to move off the shoals. The fleet met with whales again, this time off Wainwright, and a number were taken.

Five days later the wind hauled to the westward and the heavy ice was driven back. Several vessels were held helpless in the pack. Others got under way and worked in between the grounded ice and the shore, as they had done before. In the sudden change, some small boats were caught miles away from their ships. The hunters dragged their boats up on the ice and hauled them over the hummocks for miles, back to their ships.

The ice kept driving in and several vessels, helpless against it, were backed up until they grounded. The stubborn, courageous whalemen refused to give up in spite of having their ships jammed behind the ice. Helpless as they were, they continued to keep their boats in the open water, searching for whales. "The wind will soon change," they said. "It'll sweep the ice out to sea." The whales, thick in the floes, would be easy prey.

Those veterans of the ice reckoned right, for on August 25, a northeast gale broke up the ice and drove it offshore. Fair weather prevailed on August 27, and whaling went on at a lively pace as the vessels were freed from the icepack and stood toward deeper water.

Two days later, the wind hauled to the southwest, driving the ice back toward the American shore and pinning the whaleships between shore and ice. Some of the ships anchored on the shoals in four or five fathoms of water. Snow and squalls swept down.

The brigantine *Comet* was crushed September 2. Five days later the barkentine *Ramon* was crushed while its crew was cutting up a whale. The floe caught the ship on each side and crushed her like an eggshell,

Photos in this chapter courtesy of Mystic Seaport.

58

leaving not a vestige of her forty-five minutes from the time the ice first closed in.

The barkentine *Awashonka* was crushed next day, and by now there was serious concern amongst the masters. Off to seaward lay solid ice. The only open space was the strip of water along the shore behind the grounded ice. Winter was coming on. The Arctic was beginning to reach out with its frigid tentacles and when it once got the whale ships fast in its grip, there would be no chance for them to escape.

Realizing their perilous plight, the masters of the fleet held a conference to decide on a course of action. "Seventy miles down the coast are the seven vessels that separated from our fleet earlier," one skipper recalled. "They're outside the ice barrier."

"Aye," replied another master. "Could we send an expedition in a small boat to tell them of our plight?"

It was agreed.

Now, after an agonizing wait, they received word that the seven vessels would be standing by to render what assistance they could. "But what happens now?" they asked one another. "If we stay aboard our ships we will only see them crushed, with perhaps much loss of life."

It was a heartbreaking decision, but there was only one thing to do—abandon the stricken ships and head south the best way they could.

On September 14, the crews of the twenty-nine whalers abandoned their ships as they lay fast in the ice. The fleet's boats were put into the water, provisioned and equipped for the long journey. Climbing aboard them were wives, families, masters, and rugged whale hunters. The long trek began.

Skirting along the shore, the little flotilla with its several hundred people made for the open sea to the south. The first night they landed and camped on the beach. In the morning they continued their journey. A strong wind came up which created a new hazard for their overladen boats. The women prayed, the men cursed or sang, as they rowed through the churning sea, but there was no hysteria . . . no tears. For these were whalers who lived by an unwritten code of courage in the face of danger. Wives and children were equally responsible to this code. They were fine, brave sailors. This existence at sea was never easy, but it was their chosen way of life.

Icy Cape. Safety at last. The grateful group boarded the rescue vessels which took them to Plover Bay. From there, they sailed for Honolulu, Hawaii, the whalers' favorite spot for "wintering over," where all arrived safely. In all the annals of ship disasters, this story remains the most remarkable. For, in spite of the fact that an entire whaling fleet was crushed by ice, not a single life was lost.

59

Again the *Bear* went plunging through ice, which began to converge in the long, dark lead ahead of us. We could see that the pack was solid over toward Herald Island on our port beam. Flickers of light moved up and down along the wavering line which was the horizon, reflections from the ice which set off myriad filterings, sometimes colored with the magic of the spectrum.

Withdrawing from the misty distance, our eyes moved inward, and there in the sharper zone of near vision lay new wonders of this strange world. Sometimes the ice close aboard showed walls twenty feet high and brown as a country road in winter. Such ice had hit bottom, rolled over, and was now floating again. The sharp breeze that blew down off the polar sea carried a tang which bit at the lips and hands. There was always the taste of salt spray in the air. This same breeze whipped up the ice-free water into turbulent, short whitecaps, among which at times the broad flukes of a whale's tail rose as the monsters moved through the sea. Overhead, in streams, swept shadows and points of light; these were the whale-birds, thousands of them, hovering over the whale herd with a wild, wheeling rhythm all their own.

The whales disappeared beneath the ice, the lead closed in, and, as the ship drove by the solid, white ice walls, eider ducks swooped overhead in flight, now right, now left, wing tip to wing tip, up, down, over, and under—all in rhythmic unison. Our two specimen hunters were fascinated by the display. Bailey said, "Eiders are hunted for their flesh. In the old days, natives used their skins for clothing to be worn nearest the body."

Hendee interjected his knowledge. "Now, the more civilized Eskimos pluck the feathers and down for stuffing pillows and feather beds. In the south of Greenland, they make beautiful blankets and wall carpets out of eider-duck skins. It takes about a hundred skins to make a good-sized blanket."

We turned back to watch the scene. Sea pigeons whirled by in black clouds. A polar bear lounged on a field of ice but we would never have spotted him, had he not moved around from time to time.

Now our attention was drawn to a mass of moving blackness on the flat ice. "It's a herd of walrus," John Lidmann said. "They're not certain if we're friend or foe."

I watched, fascinated, as they lumbered toward the water and tumbled in with a great splash. Nearby, and completely ignored by the walrus, was a yellow-bellied whale, bottom up and quite dead.

The *Bear* rolled heavily in the swell that was kicked up in an open bit of sea. The ensign at the gaff and loose ends of rope fluttered out in a time-beating

61

tremble in the wind. Now the sails were loosed, for the wind had hauled fair and the sea was open for a spell. "Every bit of help is welcome," the Captain said, as he noted the wind and ordered that the sails be set.

"Aye, aye, Sir."

We pulled at the braces and the halyards in setting the sails. Wind stung our faces and hands as we worked in time-honored rhythm. Slush, slush, slush, went the beating chop of the propeller in a singsong consonance.

Rhythm, rhythm, rhythm! Everything around seemed inexorably attuned to some magic symphony of sound and motion. And, I told myself, surely all the world responds to the rhythms that embrace it in such a masterly oneness. The rhythm seemed to become a part of thought, leading one to see what is beyond the present, and at the same time into the past. Again I felt a bond with the men who had sailed through just such scenes so long ago. I could almost hear their voices crying for response and I desperately wanted to say, "Yes, I am here. How was it with you on Captain Cook's ship, or you on the *Jeannette,* the *Blossom,* or the *Plover?* Did you feel the magic of this same Arctic as I now do?"

I was rational enough to know that I could not go back among them, back to their world, except on the wings of fancy. Yet, I could use my imagination to be lifted into their realm. Time and space did not matter. In fancy, in dreams, I could accomplish anything, go anywhere, feel anything!

The *Bear* ran into Kotzebue Sound and anchored. An Army radio operator was put ashore in a boat for his tour of duty at a lonely inland station. It was here that Captain Cochran related the story of one of the most fantastic rescues ever made. The heroine? The *Bear* of course.

It was in the summer of 1897 that fifteen whalers went north for their annual season of hunting. Vessels coming out in the fall reported that the main part of the fleet had been caught at Point Barrow. Many of them were in danger of being crushed by the ice. Their crews had provisions to last them until December since that was the time they were expected back in San

62

Photos on pages 62 and 65, courtesy of National Geographic Magazine, © *National Geographic Society.*

Francisco. Eight ships and 265 whalemen would have to wait until the following July or August until a ship could get through the ice. They would surely starve to death or freeze.

The nation's sympathy was with the trapped unfortunates. The case seemed hopeless since no ship had ever ventured into the Arctic so late in the season. No one had ever traveled great distances across such terrain in the dead of winter. Yet, something would have to be done.

The news finally reached the White House, and President William McKinley ordered the Secretary of the Treasury to contact the Revenue Cutter Service for a possible rescue plan. Captain C. F. Shoemaker, chief of the Revenue Cutter Service, wrote to Captain Francis Tuttle of the *Bear* . . . "Would the *Bear* attempt the rescue?"

The *Bear* had just returned to Port Townsend after a summer in the North. She would have to be reprovisioned and fitted out for the Herculean task. And what about a crew? Captain Tuttle asked for volunteers. His officers and the entire crew said, almost in unison, "We'll go!"

Three weeks later, November 27, 1897, the *Bear* steamed out of Seattle and headed north. At Dutch Harbor, where she was hastily coaled, the natives expressed great concern over the proposed plans. But there was no other choice—she must go on.

It was impossible for a vessel to penetrate into the Arctic ice as far north as Point Barrow at that time of year. The only alternative was to land an expeditionary force as far north as possible. The group could carry food and aid to Point Barrow. Eighty-five miles from Cape Nome, Captain Tuttle realized he could go no farther. Reluctantly he turned back. The *Bear* crunched her way through the ice to Cape Vancouver, fighting cold and gales and granite-like ice all the way, searching for a safe place to put a relief expedition ashore.

There was supposed to be a small Eskimo village nearby. At last, as the afternoon fog lifted, Captain Tuttle spotted a group of dwellings. This was Nelson's Island, behind Nunivak. Boats hauled the provisions ashore, but it was impossible to carry large amounts of food for such distances. Another plan would have to be devised.

The relief party would have to travel by dog sled and drive a herd of reindeer ahead of them. These reindeer would provide fresh meat and warm clothing for the stranded whalers at Point Barrow.

Lieutenant David Jarvis of the *Bear* had charge of the party which set out in late December. With him were Second Lieutenant E. P. Bertholf (who was later a Coast Guard Commandant) and Dr. S. J. Call, the ship's surgeon. Also included were F. Koltchoff, an expert reindeer man, and a half-breed, Alexis Kalenin, who agreed to act as guide for the party as far as St. Michael.

The group split into two parties; Lieutenant Bertholf stayed behind to pick up some extra gear to be landed by the *Bear,* while Lieutenant Jarvis and the doctor went on ahead. There was no time to be wasted, and both parties used dog sleds with Eskimo drivers. Both groups arranged for reindeer herds to be driven north. These reindeer, ironically, had been brought to Alaska from Siberia by the *Bear's* first skipper, Captain Healy. Now they were to figure in one of the greatest rescues of all time.

The trek was a dangerous, harrowing one. From St. Michael, Lieutenant Jarvis and Dr. Call had to cross the Yukon River near its mouth, wind around Norton Sound along the shore of Golovnin Bay, and skirt the barren beach which later became Nome. Then, on to Cape Rodney.

They felt the full bite of the sub-zero weather and resorted to sleeping with the Eskimos in their huts in order to keep warm. They learned that deerskin clothing was far warmer than heavy woolens. In the morning, they roused their dogs out of the deep snowdrifts where they had burrowed and fed them dried fish or seal meat. The dogs had to be fed individually to avoid fatal fights.

All along the way they gave medical aid to the natives. They fought off wolves which attacked their dogs or reindeer herds. Sometimes a deer became lost in a blizzard and had to be left behind. The men lived on hardtack, bacon and beans, with tea. Occasionally they munched on dried apples.

At last they reached Point Barrow, after having traveled more than 1500 miles along the coast, in and out of bays and inlets, over mountains, across ice-covered bog and rivers—driving their reindeer all the way. The date was March 29, 1898. The overland trip had taken over three months.

The distressed whalers could hardly believe their eyes. Here was food, in the form of reindeer which they would slaughter, and medical care from the *Bear's* doctor. But the expedition soon realized its work had just begun, for many of the men were living aboard their battered ships in the ice. Others, whose ships had been crushed, were huddled along the shore in pitiful makeshift dwellings. It became necessary to travel miles along the beaches and out on the ice-bound ocean to visit the ships and give food and medical aid where needed.

The Eskimos all along the coast were generally good-hearted people, and those around Point Barrow gave up their reindeer skins to help clothe the stranded whalers. Charlie Brower, agent for a whaling and trading company, obliged the whalers by donating all his surplus food and supplies so that the men would survive.

The doctor found the whalers in a filthy condition, often suffering from scurvy. Many of them had lost heart, and were resigned to a kind of "living death" in misery and filth. Exhausted, often hungry and cold themselves, the rescuers worked through the entire summer of 1898.

Meanwhile, the *Bear* had returned to Dutch Harbor to winter over. Early in the spring she started north again, toward the Arctic, around Cape Prince of Wales. On July 28, she arrived off Point Barrow. Jubilant whalemen, happy Eskimos, and excited dogs raced over the ice to the ship. Never had the old *Bear* looked so beautiful. Of the 265 men from the various ships, the *Bear* brought ninety-seven back to the States.

By some lucky chance, the *Bear* went back along the coast near Point Hope, and there she found the trading schooner *Louise J. Kennedy* stranded and rolled over in the surf, her crew cast on the shore. Here was yet another group to rescue as she headed southward.

"Yes," Captain Cochran said. "That was quite a busy season all right." He should know, for he was the lanky lieutenant who navigated the *Bear*. All these years he had come back to the Arctic because he loved the Northland with its ice, fog, walrus, whales, and

spotted seals. He even loved the squatty, moon-faced Eskimos who still looked upon him, through their red, snow-burned eyes, as a sort of god of the sea.

Sometimes storytelling sessions on the *Bear* included Dr. Sturdevant, when he wasn't ashore with his bag of tools, pills, and medicines. Once he brought me an old journal, the record kept by Dr. Call of the *Bear* in 1897. "Read this," he said. "You'll get a good picture of the medical aid that shipmasters gave to the people up here twenty years ago."

In spare moments I read through the journal, to the tune of creaking, groaning timbers, by the light of the swaying overhead lantern. I felt the thrill of association with this man whose deeds I was sharing.

June 25, 1897, at 9:30 a.m. I set out on a sick call to the *Belevedere* lying in the ice sixty miles to the southward. My equipment consisted of five dogs and and a sled carrying our sleeping bags, food, medicine, shotgun, and ammunition. There being no snow on the land, we were compelled to take to the ice along the coast. The past warm weather, melting snow and breaking out the lakes and lagoons, had covered the shore ice with water and broken it up to such an extent that our progress was slow and the work very hard. We were three days in reaching the ship.

Captain Millard had improved greatly since our arrival on the 26th of March. . . . Remaining three days there, I left on the morning of June 30, and after another four days of hauling through the rain and sleet, arrived at Point Barrow July 13.

So much for Dr. Call himself. His notes continued, however, with words of praise for the captains of the whaling fleet. One such man was Captain George B. Leavitt, whose notes conjured up many of the less romantic aspects of whaling.

I am glad to have the dates of most of the amputations since the ships began wintering at Herschel Island. The first was on a man belonging to the *Mary D. Hume* in March, 1891. Half the right foot was taken off, the instruments used being a butcher knife and a hacksaw. Captain Tilton bossed the job.

It was the first attempt of the kind up there and putting the patient under chloroform (which was out of my line) was a slow process. We placed the bottle under the man's nose and after he had taken a whiff, we would ask him if he were sleepy. This was kept up for half an hour, without effect. We

then made a paper cone, put in some waste saturated with chloroform, and the man went right off.

It was a cut square across the foot. After cutting, the edges were drawn together as far as they would come, with gauze well-greased placed over the cut, followed by absorbent cotton saturated with Friar's balsam. . . .

March 9, 1894. Both feet, or the best part of both feet, were amputated from a man belonging to the *Narwhal*. These feet were taken off well back, the same way as with the other amputations, with the difference that after the foot was cut to the bone, a piece of canvas was put on and the flesh hauled back and the bones then cut off. In this way, a flap was formed and the whole business turned out very well.

December 9, 1894. Six fingers and three toes were amputated from a man belonging to the *Thrasher*. Captain Tilton was the head surgeon while Bodfish and myself were assistants.

December 28, 1895. Amputated a finger from the hand of Mr. Tilton, the second mate of the *Alexander*.

February 3, 1896. Amputated a finger from a man belonging to the *Jeanette*.

February 17, 1896. Amputated a part of one foot from a man belonging to the *Beluga*. From the time this man was put under the influence of chloroform until he came to, only thirty minutes intervened. Iodoform was the only antiseptic I used in all my surgery.

My next big contract was taking off the right arm of Mr. Best, the third officer of the *Narvarch,* on June 20, 1896. The arm was amputated a few inches below the shoulder, cleaning off all the burnt flesh. In putting a ligature on the large artery, gut was used. The small veins were touched with caustic. After bandaging the arm, a compress was kept on, in case of accident, until the ligature was removed. On the 28th of June I had to make a second operation, this time laying open the whole shoulder and taking the bone off within an inch of the joint. Disarticulation, as I understand it, meaning unjointed. Well, I did not do that, but left, I should say, one inch clear of the joint.

Well, thought I, what a fantastic breed of men—both the patients and the "doctors." I wondered if I would ever have the courage to take another man's life in my hands, and somehow manage to save it under such primitive conditions.

Those were cruel days for any patient. I was quite content to be where I was—aboard the *Bear* in 1921 with a qualified medical doctor on board.

Chapter Eleven : Her Name Was Susie

The *Bear* passed along the coast skirting Cape Espenberg, passed Kivalina, Cape Seppings and Cape Thompson. In the misty distance ahead lay the headlands around Point Hope. Ice began to appear, the waters to shoal.

"Better start sounding with the hand lead," said Captain Cochran quietly.

The leadsman stepped into the chains, swung his heavy leads, and began his systematic calling to the bridge, "No bottom at ten."

The pilothouse clock showed the hour's end. I ran along the boat deck and tapped out the time on that old Secor bell, "Bong, bong . . . bong, bong." Then I went aft to take a machine sounding with a glass tube. I dipped up a canvas bucket full of sea water and took the temperature. It was all routine, even to the part where Thor appeared on the quarterdeck, began to run around in spasmodic circles, and whine pitifully. He was having one of his fits which no doctor had yet been able to help.

"Dog on the Q.D.!" cried the boatswain's mate.

"Chu-u-g-g-!" came the thumping of the ship as we hit a heavier bit of ice. Now we could hear the familiar scraping sound as the white stuff slid along the ship's side.

On the bridge, Captain Cochran pointed toward the land. "Just about in there," he said, "we ran in to pick up the crew of the schooner *Louise J. Kenny* when she wrecked."

"No bottom at ten," interrupted the leadsman from the chains below.

Dr. Sturdevant came down from the bridge to check his handbag for medicines and instruments before going ashore at Point Hope.

Our journey continued along the icy shores until at last we arrived at the Eskimo village of Wainwright. It was here that we met Susie, siren of the North.

She came off from shore in a walrus-skin umiak which was loaded to the water's edge with about thirty Eskimos, all bent on trade. The minute we spotted her, we knew there was something different about this girl. Perhaps it was the confident way in which she flung her head back as she climbed the sea ladder. That, along with the fillip of her parka hood as it lay back on her exposed shoulders, gave her a kind of jaunty sophistication not seen in the others of her tribe.

The calico covering the outside of her fur parka was bright red; her mukluks of a gayer pattern than the others. Her beads were shinier and more neatly sewn on, and the wolf fringe of her parka hood stood out in a wider ring around her face. Her hair was jet black against the brown of her full cheeks, and her eyes flashed with an eager interest in everything about us—and about the *Bear*. There was not a trace of timidity or fear.

"How old do you suppose she is?" Happy whispered, his eyes popping out of his head. Any minute he would ask her to dance. But no . . . I realized that Happy had suddenly become bashful.

"About twenty," I answered, appraising this girl from a far-off land as sailors traditionally do. Strangely enough, she did not evoke whistles but rather awed, incredulous gazes from the *Bear's* passengers and crew. Surely she was aware that she possessed some rare, indescribable quality known only to the fascinating temptresses of history, for soon she was nodding to Mr. Parker and nonchalantly asking him for a cigarette.

Flustered as he was, he produced one and lit it for her. "Thank you," she said, smiling in secret amusement. "What is your name?"

"Parker," he said with effort.

"Mine is Susie."

She turned her back on him to walk around the quarterdeck and look down on the men gazing adoringly from the well. She gave them a coquettish smile. This, coming from a seemingly wild little girl from the ice country, was unbelievable. Had not the men of the *Bear* dealt with hundreds of her people in a kindly, patronizing way? Yet, this one girl, Susie, had charmed the entire ship in a matter of minutes.

Now, she turned and smiled at me. I braced myself, determined to muster every ounce of military bearing. I smiled back as she walked over and stood beside me.

"My name is Susie," she said. Deep dimples formed in her cheeks as she spoke. She spoke good, understandable English. Surely her racial strain was mixed with white.

"Yes, I heard you introduce yourself. My name is Ransom."

"I am happy to be aboard the *Bear*. We look forward to such visits from the outside world. Do you like it here in Alaska?"

Except for the clothing and the setting, our conversation could have occurred anywhere in the world between two people who were interested in one another. "I like it very much," I said. "I hope we will be stopping here again on the way back from Demarcation Point."

"Oh," she said with delight, her eyes sparkling with happy plans. "I will make you mukluks with beads on them." She held up a foot to show the bootee-like covering. "Like these."

"They are the most beautiful I have ever seen," I told her quite honestly.

"Then you will see me again?"

"Oh yes."

"Good." She adjusted her parka hood. "Now I must go trade with my family." She started away, then turned. "Ransom . . . would you do something for me?"

Mesmerized, I answered, "If I possibly can, Susie."

"Write me a letter. I have never had a letter and I know that others receive them once a year. I would like sometime to have a letter from the outside. I would keep it all my life."

"Of course, Susie. I will write to you."

As I watched her move along the deck I felt a strange incantation drumming in my brain, born, no doubt, of that compounding magic of Ulysses and Calypso. To me, for the moment, there was no gray sky, no mud-smeared ice rolled up on the beach of the most desolate place in the world.

No, none of these. For now I understood about all the adventurers who had ever stood upon strange beaches, seen strange sights, and heard strange chants. For I had met my very own Circe. At that moment, there was not another important thing in all the wide, wide world.

Trading was in full sway. As with elsewhere, it became a repetition of what had gone on before. Carved ivory, here, was the best of the native art.

In the long winter days, the carvers spent innumerable hours bent over their toil. Considering the tools used and the conditions of their labor, they came up with some remarkable pieces, many of which, by now, decorated mantles and curio cabinets in thousands of faraway homes.

Cribbage boards abounded. But how would an Eskimo with no factory-made drills or precise measuring devices create such a board out of solid ivory? To accomplish this feat, they made spindles of wood with sharpened nail ends, and, as an Indian or Boy Scout might start a fire, they whirled these round and round until holes were drilled into the hard ivory. Then, with a broken pocketknife blade filed as a hook, they scratched decorative lines on the surface. They pictured all the Arctic life they knew, such as whales, fish, seal, and bear, and even such ships as called in the North. Then they blackened the designs with soot and polished the tusk until it gleamed.

These patient craftsmen carved tiny models of their Arctic animals, and built exquisite little ship models with ivory masts, yards, and sails. Since the old men knew and remembered the whale ships, they carved that type of vessel, leaving newer types to the younger generation.

The *Bear* was one of the most copied of all ships. Every Eskimo had seen the *Bear*. One Eskimo who came on board stood on the deck of the *Bear*, holding up his miniature of the ship. He waved his arm around the ship, then pointed to his model for comparison, willing to swap it for calico, knives, tobacco, or food. It was a beautiful work of art and was soon on display in the wardroom.

Hour after hour these people had labored, giving each detail the skill and the patience that any artist the wide world over, throughout the ages, must give to his work in order to make it truly fine. I thought how basically alike artists must be—how similar they were in spirit to the ancient Greek sculptors.

One of the Eskimos who came on board to trade gave a personal demonstration of the artist-at-work. Squatting on the quarterdeck of the *Bear,* with legs crossed and body hunched forward, he scratched, gouged, and polished the ivory tusk. As he worked, he swayed back and forth, chanting weirdly in unison with the other Eskimos who, among themselves, had been coaxed into performing one of their tribal dances. Here, before our eyes, we learned that the spirit of the actor lived in the hearts of those simple people, no differently than it did in our own.

Trading for ivory was in full sway.

We had one more task to perform at Wainwright, and that was disembarking the new teacher, Mr.

69

Ward. "I've never seen anybody so excited as that fellow is," Happy LaRue said. "He's had his gear packed for hours."

"And he was first in the whaleboat for a look-see at his new home," I added. "Here he comes now for his gear."

Our prim Mr. Ward, in the three hours he'd spent ashore making friends with his new students, was a completely changed man. Dressed in an Eskimo parka that smelled of walrus blubber, it was almost impossible to distinguish between pupil and teacher. Now, the umiak came alongside and Mr. Ward bounded on board, chattering happily with his new friends as they gathered up his gear.

He barely had time to wave goodbye to the *Bear* as he leaped back into the umiak beside the natives, seized a paddle, and helped them splash away toward shore.

In another hour Mr. Ward was forgotten, and the *Bear* steamed on for that spot that had become a sort of symbol of Alaska's far frontier, Point Barrow.

"No bottom at ten!" called the leadsman.

Point Barrow was low and flat. About five hundred people lived there and we were certain that all of them, along with their running, yelping dogs, had come out to see us.

The first boat ashore took Mr. Watkins and his box of instruments. "We'll stay for two days," Captain Cochran said. "Long enough for him to make his observations."

There would be time also for the two "birdmen" to land and take specimens. I could not help noticing a sigh of resignation from the Captain as he anticipated the next few days. Those men would be skinning birds and scraping bones all over the deck, boxing and bagging items for the Denver museum. Ah, well. . . .

Despite a moderate offshore gale and a choppy sea, we went ahead landing our passengers and freight. There were the school teacher and his wife, the Presbyterian missionary, the doctor for the hospital, and his wife and little boy. There was also a nurse who would remain at the Point Barrow hospital for the next four years.

"What are the chances of trading with the natives?" I asked John Lidmann. I was anxious to collect articles from each port we visited, and so far had nothing from Point Barrow.

"Not good," he answered. "The *Herman* and *Lady Kindersley* have beat us to the trade goods on this trip."

I was feeling a bit sorry for myself when I heard the commotion of a huge umiak coming alongside. Standing in the center of it, surrounded by two dozen Eskimos all pulling, yelling, and laughing, was a white man who swung in under the counter of the *Bear* and climbed the sea ladder.

"Well, Charlie! Good to see you, man." Captain Cochran shook his hand heartily. "By golly, you haven't changed a bit in all these years."

"Yup," Charlie said. "This here's the life for me."

This was the man I had been hearing about for years—Charlie Brower!

I noticed a wink and a nudge from the Captain, as the two of them disappeared into the cabin to talk and perhaps liven their words with the relaxing medicinal stimulant taken from one of the doctor's bottles labeled, strangely enough, "White Horse."

John Lidmann explained Charlie's presence at Point Barrow. "He's king of the tribe around these parts. Landed here from a whaler a generation ago, married a native, and raised a family. It was he who broke out the stores of supplies for the stranded whalers in 1898 and assisted the *Bear* on her famous trip that year." He shook his head. "Not many men left like old Charlie."

For those of us who could not get ashore for a run on the beach, there was always a feeling of discontent. Confinement over such a long period of time was bound to give us the feeling that we were living in a museum—the *Bear*—and that we were the specimens. Happy LaRue, the loudest grumbler of all, somehow managed to turn our gloom to comedy.

"Come on. I'm tired of reindeer meat, day in and day out." He eyed the grunting hog that we had been carrying since we'd left Unalaska. He beckoned it with his finger. "Here piggy, piggy. . . . This little piggy went to market." Creeping stealthily towards those luscious pork chops, he continued his meaningful chant. "This little piggy stayed home. But *this little piggy . . .!*"

Needless to say, we thoroughly enjoyed our chow that night. It was delicious in spite of the fact that the hog had matured on a diet of garbage and coal.

Diaries, ship names, records of people—all these came together as would the pieces of a fantastic and marvelous puzzle. My wonder never ceased, as I read, observed, listened, and lived aboard the *Bear*. Kipling talked about that "touch of the sun." Arctic voyagers referred to that strange state of mind as "ice blink." Others said it was "madness" which made people think and see and do things of greatness or foolishness. I sometimes wondered if there were something wrong with me since I so thoroughly enjoyed this strange life. Yet, I reasoned, I was too old to be accused of childishness and too young for senility.

I shrugged my shoulders and cinched up the hood of my parka. There would never be an answer to that one, except perhaps one day when I was very old and could sit back before a roaring fire and put my feet up. I could swap tales with the best of 'em, and I could tell the youngsters a thing or two. Yes, there was a reward to look forward to, a kind of insurance for the days when I could no longer sail the Arctic seas. . . .

With this in mind, I was more faithful than ever to my diary. "August 11, 1921," I wrote. "The *Bear* dropped anchor in the midst of heavy ice after a strenuous night of steaming through miles of slack ice. We did not penetrate the vast fields of solid white, for to do so would have meant imprisonment.

"There are only three or four fathoms of water under us. It is impossible to go ahead. Low-lying land is visible beyond the white hummocks several miles away. A small two-masted schooner lies in the ice between the *Bear* and shore. Along the shore are several huts and a flagpole.

"Last night and this morning were mostly foggy, blown clear at times by strong northeasterly winds. Barometer is high—30.30—but the temperature has fallen to freezing. The solid pack ice which we passed this morning extends for miles to the north of us and is the heaviest we have seen thus far. Shortly after noon, the fog lifted to disclose a flat piece of land ahead of us. I was told it was called Cross Island.

"At one point, a sounding with hand lead showed a depth of less than three fathoms. The island seems little farther than a quarter of a mile away on our starboard beam although we know it is many leagues away. Thus, the misty air deceives us.

"The ice is broken into heavy chunks sticking out of the water; one foot, twenty, twenty-five feet and much of it appears to be grounded. Some of it which has rolled over shows mud on the bottom."

The *Bear* soon weighed anchor and proceeded on. "Cross Island," declared Captain Cochran. "That's where the whaler *Reindeer* was crushed in the ice in 1894. That two-masted schooner over there," he pointed, "that's the ex-sealer *Olga*."

Now John Lidmann told us of the days he had sailed this area in the *Jeannie* before joining the *Bear*. "Then there was the *Karluk*. She was wrecked in a fatal ice drift in 1913. Captain Bartlett was her skipper. . . ."

"Wasn't that the same man who, in 1909, commanded the *Roosevelt* for Commodore Peary when he made his dash for the North Pole?"

"That's right," John said. "And it's too bad that the skipper's later trip was so grim. Some of the men from the *Karluk* got to Wrangel, but there were four others," he nodded towards Herald Island, "who are no doubt lying there frozen, to this day."

"And Bartlett. Did he get out?" I asked.

"Yes. He walked over the ice to the Asian mainland and followed the coast to East Cape. From there he got passage to Nome."

Again I wondered aloud how whalers in those old and cruel days managed to lure men to sign on board as crews.

"Lure!" hooted Speechley. He was hanging on to one of the shrouds abreast the galley door, sipping coffee which he had scrounged from the cook. "Well, let me tell you. . . ."

Others of the "lower deck" crowded around to listen, for they had all been talking about whalers getting iced in. This was a subject pertinent to the moment since the *Bear* could get iced in just as the *Thetis* had at Herschel Island. "The *Thetis* was investigating whalers there. In doing so, they found a sailor who asked for passage back to the States. Turned out he'd been shanghaiied two years before."

"No foolin'?"

"That's right," Speechley confided. "I got the story straight from the boarding officer. Anyway, this man was a boatswain's mate in the U. S. Navy. He'd gone ashore from his ship in San Francisco, and headed for the local pub. When he woke up, he found himself headed out the Golden Gate in a whaler."

"Well, I'll be! What'd he do about it?"

Speechley shrugged. "What could he do? He went aft and said to the captain, 'I want to be taken back!' And the captain says, 'Can you steer?' 'Aye,' says the boatswain's mate. 'Then take the wheel.' Just like that. And for two years he continued to take the wheel in his regular turn, against his will."

"Did the *Thetis* take him back to San Francisco?"

"Oh sure," said Speechley. He curled his lips at the irony of the situation. "And he wound up as defendant in a general court-martial for desertion from the Navy. I heard he got out of it all right, though." He turned to go below, then glanced back over his shoulder. "Does that answer your question about how some of the whalers were manned?"

The *Bear* plodded on through the night, the lessening light fading into the shadows over the ice around us. The fog swept by and clung to the mast, yards, and rigging, turning into a crystal covering.

Each time the *Bear* hit the ice with a crunching thud, part of the frozen jacket flew off in a thousand white particles and clattered down on the deck with a frosty crackle. John Lidmann was earning his pay this night, for every shock of impact sent him slipping around in the lofty crow's nest until I could almost hear his teeth rattle. The wind increased from the northeast and set the pack harder down on us. The *Bear* poked her nose in here and there, as John shouted his orders to the helmsman.

The ice got higher, and soon we could see a solid wall of it as high as the deck of the ship. Massive hummocks had piled one upon another until they merged into the mist.

Now the ship moved in a narrow channel of her own making with the ice quickly closing in astern. When the ship hit the ice, the engines were always stopped at the moment of impact, with the propeller

Courtesy of U. S. Coast Guard

blades in vertical position so as not to be caught or broken by the ice.

But suddenly the propeller stuck, caught by heavy blue ice. We were stuck fast.

Banks of fog swept in thicker overhead, and we could see nothing. When it cleared we found ourselves in a shadowy half-light, shivering in the eerie coldness. A lost seabird swooped and screamed. Captain Cochran paced the bridge in his reindeer coat, squinting ahead, astern, off to the north. He seemed concerned but not alarmed. In spite of his irritable manner, his eyes gleamed with joy. He was fighting the enemy again. The driving wind, if it persisted, could force the ice to the shore and we would be trapped in it. True, it was August, but if the ice were grounded, the *Bear* would be right along with it. But if the wind let up or swung around to the opposite direction it could clear the sea in a few minutes.

Now the wind dropped to a light air, then died entirely. A low, rumbling noise came over the ice. The deep, white encircling wall seemed to rise and fall in the motion set up by the water.

"Send a man aloft," ordered the Captain.

John Lidmann, parka hood encasing his face, steam blowing from his lips, leaped into the shrouds and raced up the ratlines. He too seemed to be filled with a strange joy. He was in his element, for had he not often done this aboard the *Jeannie?*

Aloft, he leaned out over the edge of the crow's nest, a ghostlike figure high above the deck.

"There! There on the port bow!" he called out in an urgent voice.

To the northward, darkness showed. The pressure of ice was slackening off. Leads began to open out. The *Bear* backed the length of her tiny lake of freedom, went full ahead, climbed up on the edge of her confinement, and came down with a crunch. She broke through the heaviest shoulder of ice, and began to move slowly ahead.

The dark streak forward widened. We had found a good lead at last! The flat ice spread wide before us. Backing, filling, cutting right, then left into the leads, we continued on until we cleared the barrier that cut us off from the waters around Demarcation Point.

Captain Cochran grunted with relief, then disappeared into his sea cabin for a nap.

The crack of rifle shots broke the Arctic silence that foggy morning of August 13. There was a lull, then several more shots. The *Bear's* engines stopped. From the bridge, we peered toward the unseen shore. A repeat fusillade gave us a better bearing.

"That's one good way of attracting attention," I said to John.

"It's about the only way, up here where you can't see very far." He pointed toward the shoreline about a half a mile away. A boat under sail was sliding out of the mist, in an attempt to overtake us. The breeze was slight and contrary. "It'll take them a good half hour to reach us at the rate they're going," he said.

The boat proved to be a New Bedford-type whaleboat, perhaps one left or lost by some ancient whaleship, for the sails were much tattered from long use. As we watched, it tacked back and forth again and again before it could fetch up at our gangway. A white man and a dozen Eskimos looked up at us and grinned. The entire scene reminded me of Charlie Brower back at Point Barrow as wife, children, uncles, aunts, and cousins all streamed aboard.

The central figure, wearing reindeer skins and sealskin breeches, was as brown and grizzly-looking as the others. "Well, well, Captain Cochran. It's been a mighty long time. . . ." The two men shook hands, then walked aft to the taffrail to talk, as old friends will after a long separation.

The remainder of the boatload began trading the few things they had brought, but it was a poor offering. They had already disposed of their last winter's collection to the traders *Herman* and *Lady Kindersley*. "They beat us again," Happy said, remembering Wainwright. We learned that the traders had gone on to Herschel Island.

The Captain returned with his old friend and bid him goodbye at the gangway. "You say we're about forty miles from Demarcation Point?"

"Yup," he said, putting an affectionate hand on the Captain's shoulder. "Take care of yourselves and keep the lead line going. We wouldn't want anything to happen to the *Bear*."

Happy looked at me. His jaw dropped. "Do you suppose he knows something we don't know?"

I laughed. "I'm sure if he does, he's already told the Captain."

Again we merged into the mists, sounding with the lead line and with the foghorn blowing, as the law required. A little later, in a clear moment, we sighted a group of huts on a low flat of land. A boat was heading off, this time a large umiak, again filled with a motley array of people, including a white man browned by ice and fog-filtered winds until he was nut-colored. He climbed the ladder to joyfully seize

75

the Captain's hand; then they disappeared aft.

We learned that both the *Herman* and the *Lady Kindersley* had preceded us. Those two vessels began to loom in our thoughts as a pair of fast-roving claim jumpers, each trying to get ahead of the other: the *Lady Kindersley* for the Hudson's Bay Company and the *Herman* for Liebes and Company, furriers of San Francisco. They reminded me of the Phoenicians and the Norsemen who turned up wherever profit was to be had, bringing civilization with them.

Now a boy of eighteen or twenty leaped out from among the Eskimos to climb aboard after the white man. We could not help noticing the respect all the Eskimos had for this English-speaking boy, as he moved among them like a leader. He grinned with good humor and reached out his hand to any of us who would take it, then pointed aft, "He is my father. His name is Gordon and he is the Liebes and Company agent."

"Well, that explains a great deal," I said. "But where did you learn to speak such fine English?"

"I have been to school in San Francisco," he answered proudly. The group of Eskimos noaded like doting parents. "We are sorry that the traders have taken all our furs. We have nothing much for you."

"So we have heard," Happy said resignedly and turned away.

I was intrigued by the young man's story, and hoped he would tell me more about his father. With a bit of friendly prompting, he did.

"My father came here in 1888. He was nineteen when he ran away from the whaler and he has been here ever since."

. . . 1888! That was another of those years of whaleship disasters, like the one in 1897-8, and the greater one of 1871. I pictured the boy's father, a young Scot, as he must have been when he came ashore from a stranded whaler. Gordon had stayed on, married a native girl, and was obviously very happy in this strange, outlandish place. Besides, now there was a spot bearing his name marked on the map of that distant coastline. Not many men were so honored.

The *Bear* moved on. Demarcation Point, our destination, was only five miles ahead. This was the boundary line between Alaska and Canada and, for us, the "top of the hill"—the *Ultima Thule*—the end of the line. This was what we had gone through so many weeks of painstaking navigation, personal discomfort, bad weather, and ice to achieve. And what was there at Demarcation Point? Nothing.

No town. No buildings. No lights. No brass band, no wives, or sweethearts hailing us from the dock. In fact, there was no dock, not even a few Eskimos to welcome us.

Demarcation Point was a stretch of barren land that reached far into the sea, the boundary between Alaska and Canada. Even in August, ice still clung to it. I had never seen so lonely a place in my life. The silence was overpowering.

Down went the anchor with a rattle of chain that broke the silence. "Away the whaleboat!"

"Up oars!"

"Let fall!"

The gray-hulled boat shot away towards shore. There, in the stern, sat Mr. Watkins, ready to pitch his pup tent on the dismal shore. Although we could not see him crawl into his tiny hiding place, we knew he would soon settle down happily amidst his instruments. The ice, the ship, the boat crew, and the world outside would be forgotten until he had completed his observations and it was time to leave.

The *Bear* cruised alongshore several miles to swing ship for deviation. Lieutenant Eberly, the navigator, took charge of the operation, as Captain Cochran had gone below for a nap. It was fascinating to watch this soft-mannered, scientifically precise man as he worked out his deviation table. He was determined to bring the *Bear* back to anchorage with exact precision. At a crucial moment, Lieutenant Todd relieved Lieutenant Eberly.

"All right, Bill," said Lieutenant Todd, "I've got her. Don't worry."

"Oh, I'm not worried. But. . . ."

Lieutenant Todd gestured with a sweep of his arm. "It's clear now. I can see where we're going. We won't hit that continent over there, I promise."

"Well," replied Lieutenant Eberly skeptically, "remember, its got to be the exact spot."

The *Bear* steamed back well inside the ice and anchored in seven fathoms. Ice was all around us, some

The Bear *at Demarcation Point. Ice was all around us* . . . .

of which was grounded. The wind and sea began moving it about. Soon, we were forced to raise anchor and break out between the grounded ice before we dared anchor again.

I knew Captain Cochran would be angry, but who, we wondered, would be the target for his ire? We soon learned.

"Mr. Todd!" he thundered as he strode across the deck, his reindeer coat flaring out with the breeze. "You should know better than to cruise inside the ice!"

The rest of us, not wishing to be "next," made ourselves scarce.

I went topside with my diary, started writing. "The sun goes slowly down the sky, not abruptly as in southern latitudes. The sea around us cannot throw off the oily calmness of its surface. The shore cannot shuck the white piping that reaches out for miles in both directions.

"The Arctic pack to the northward sends off its silent sheen. Between the pack and the shore lies a film of open, purple water. Soon the sun will set slightly west of north and, a little later, will rise slightly to the east of that same north. A few weeks earlier, the sun would not have set at all!"

The thought was fascinating. We were truly in the land of the midnight sun. I felt as though something were gripping the whole world round about, including everything and everyone within it. The grip was tight, and would not let go. It was oppressive, yet at the same time lifted one up.

Through the sameness of the ensuing three days, we looked at charts to pass time. They were imprinted with scores of names we recognized. Herschel Island lay fifty miles east. "That's where the *Herman* and *Lady Kindersley* are right now," said Happy enviously. "They're getting all the furs and whalebone before we get there."

"But no ivory," I consoled, remembering that walrus did not, as a rule, come east of Point Barrow in great numbers.

We talked about the *Thetis,* wintering there at Herschel Island. "Say, wouldn't it be something to get iced in there?" said Speechley. "I wouldn't mind."

John Lidmann put in his thought. "Maybe we could run on up there while Mr. Watkins is finishing his observations here."

"Sure," said Paddy. "There's plenty of canned grub in the hold."

But we all knew this was useless talk. Captain Cochran would have no part of such a scheme. He was becoming a bit irritated with the little scientist. This, of course, was a good topic for gossip in the crew's quarters.

"Say, did you hear that when the food was sent ashore in a basket for Mr. Watkins, the Captain sent word for him to pack up his gear and get back here?"

"No," Happy whispered. "What happened then?"

"Mr. Watkins sent word back that he wouldn't be finished until tomorrow."

"Ho, ho," chuckled our prankster. "That little seal must have a lot of power behind him to get away with barking at the Bull Walrus."

Captain Cochran grew more irritated by the hour at the delay caused by Mr. Watkins. Much of his impatience must have been backed by his sensitivity to our feelings, for there was nothing for us to do aboard ship except stare at the bleak expanse and talk enviously of those two traders at Herschel Island. Finally he said, "All off-watch crewmen can go ashore for a run on the tundra."

This was what we had been waiting for. Even Paddy, for an excuse, took the final lunch for Mr. Watkins ashore. Lidmann, the coxswain, steered the boat. Happy leaped in and seized an oar, as did the others. "I'm going to look for specimens," Lieutenant Todd said, remembering his dream of making a fortune in mining.

Thus manned, the whaleboat headed in through the small ice and finally reached the solid crush alongshore. Leaving a man to watch the boat, the rest of us headed for the pup tent which had been set up near the border monument.

It was hard to think of Mr. Watkins as being our villain as he crawled out of his tent to greet us. "Here, have a look at these instruments," he said happily, his slight breath sending up puffs of white steam. "I am getting excellent results."

We obediently admired his work although none of us had any idea of what he was up to. "Will you be finished soon?" Happy asked.

"Oh yes. In just a little while. I have one more observation. . . ."

79

I glanced around for Lieutenant Todd, but he had already disappeared over a hump of land. Happy and I decided to explore although there wasn't much for non-scientists to see. We caught sight of Thor several times as he loped across the soggy terrain. "I wonder what he's chasing," I said. "There's not much wild life up here."

"Oho!" Happy laughed out loud as he sprinted forward. He was after something, but what? I followed, and soon I saw him crouch down on hands and knees and reach into a small hole. Then he gathered whatever it was into his gloved hands.

I was tired from the run, but wildly curious. Was Happy suffering from a touch of iceblink? "Come on. Let me see."

He parted his thumbs just wide enough for the lemming to poke its whiskered nose out. It blinked its beady eyes in fright. "Now, don't you be afraid," Happy soothed. He was like a kid with a new puppy instead of a man with a rodent. Now he parted his hands so that I could have a better look at his new pet. It was about five inches long, with furry feet, small ears and, unlike *rattus rattus,* the common, everyday rat, this circumpolar fellow had a short tail.

"What are you going to call him?" I asked, as Happy poked his pet into his pocket. We thought about it on the way back to the boat where we would wait for Mr. Todd. "Pete . . . Charley . . . Joe . . . Milton . . .?"

"What if it's a girl?" I suggested.

Happy stopped. "I've got it! Susie." He looked at me impishly while I bristled. None of the crew had forgotten my interest in that little Wainwright maid.

"Call it Lenny. That could be either boy or girl. Lenny the Lemming. How's that?"

Happy pondered, peeked into his pocket, then nodded. "Lenny it is."

There on the top of the continent we could talk, talk, talk, for there was nothing else to do while we waited for Mr. Todd. In the past our forecastle talk had been full of gripes, but now we were momentarily free of the monotony of quarters. As usual, our talk centered on ships and the men who sailed in them. We reviewed the names of men and ships which marked the charts thereabouts: the *Plover,* the *Thetis,* and the *Beaufort Lagoon,* from which name came the Beaufort Sea; the McClure Islands were named for the McClure Expedition; Beechey Point after Beechey—men and ships who had hunted for Sir John Franklin. And there was Camden Bay, named for Bernard Camden, a junior officer of the *Bear* during her trip to the North in 1897.

Looking over the rolling tundra to the southeast, we talked of those whaling men who had deserted their ships while wintering at Thetis Bay on Herschel Island during the Klondike gold rush. Said John Lidmann, "Those men set out over the hills to join the rush for gold, but the mates of the whale ships followed after them. There were some bloody battles. A few men were wounded, and some froze to death in the ice."

Speechley cut in, "And what about the men who had to have their arms or legs cut off by sea doctors or whaling captains? Brrrr," he shuddered. "The articles signed by those men for long voyages really meant business."

"We're pretty lucky on the *Bear,*" I said in all sincerity. "Sure, we get bored, but we're on a great ship."

"Blooey!" said the fisherlad. "She's so old and rotten she'll fall apart some day."

"I don't see what's so great about the *Bear,*" piped up another lad. "Now, you just compare her to the *Maud,* or the *Gjoa.* . . ."

Said Speechley, "You've got to admire the sailors on those old whale ships. They really did something for their pay."

"You take the *Herman,*" chimed in a newcomer to the conversation. "She beats 'em all. Yes, she's some ship."

John Lidmann stuck to his old deepwater sailships. There was the *Flying Cloud,* the *James Baines,* the *Cutty Sark,* and the *Glory of the Seas.* "All those salmon ships were great, too. For instance, I knew the Swedish ship, the *Vega.* She drifted west to east across the top of Asia forty years ago. . . ." Lidmann rolled his quid of snuff around in his cheek, while his audience considered his sage words.

Happy LaRue broke the spell. "You're all crazy. No ships are famous except for the men who sail them."

About this time, Lieutenant Todd climbed around a

hummock of ice. "Come on, boys," he called cheerily. "Let's get back to the most famous ship in the world."

"Yeah!" we chorused. "Let's go out and get some more reindeer meat."

Soon the boat was out of the grounded ice and the floating cakes. Just as we approached the *Bear's* counter, the lemming squirmed free of Happy's pocket. "Lenny, come back!" he shouted, as the little creature leaped overboard and began to swim straight out to sea. Seemingly, with no sense of direction, it headed for the North Pole and disappeared amidst a gathering of porridge ice which the currents were whirling around.

I didn't like the look on Happy's face. "That's too bad," was all I could think of.

"Aw, forget it."

Mr. Watkins came on board when he had completed his experiments. Berg heaved the anchor out of the sea, and Mr. Eberly laid out a westerly course on the chart.

Well into the eight-to-twelve watch, Lieutenant Todd rang the engine room telegraph. "Half ahead!" Then, shortly, it was "Full ahead!" To the wheelman he said, "Steer course two-seven-zero."

Lidmann and part of his watch busied themselves securing the whaleboat just hoisted. Captain Cochran, looking aft from the bridge rail, suddenly growled, "Tell the boatswain's mate to clean up that mess on the poop." Poor Thor was running in circles and whining. The cabin boy was chasing him and cursing.

"Dog on the quarterdeck!" the quartermaster yelled, as he ran aft to stream the log.

Thus did we start homeward around Point Barrow. I kept thinking about Happy's lemming, and that awful look of disappointment when it leaped overboard. That little brown handful of fun . . . how was its soft, furry body faring in the frigid water? I wondered too about what kind of rat courage burned in its heart as it made its reckless plunge to freedom.

In the starless night at the top of the world, one could believe in a Demarcation Point—an *Ultima Thule*—even for rats.

The *Bear,* southbound, lay off Point Hope. Around the ship, from where we stood, Eskimos were racing and chasing one another in their umiaks. This was the last time they would see their Coast Guard friends for another year, and they made the most of it. Water splashed high as paddles dipped into the sea. They called to one another, then shouted to us.

"Something's going on here," Happy said. "Seems like they're a little too excited."

"We'll soon know," I said, as three men and a woman climbed aboard for transportation to Nome, our next port of call. We soon learned that they were to be witnesses on a murder case. An Eskimo boy had killed a missionary and the question was, had the boy been provoked or was he insane?

The traveling federal court which circulated throughout the Territory would have to decide the issue, once we deposited the witnesses at Nome. We could not help but wonder about the boy's fate, since many of these cases in the past had been complicated to the point where neither a strictly black nor white answer could be given. Now, all we could do was watch the noisy Eskimos in their umiaks, paddling back and forth beneath our sea ladder, chattering with excited concern. Suddenly, they swung around and raced madly for shore.

"Hey, what's this!" Happy pointed to a new center of activity.

I turned to see half the crew circling a woman who had just come aboard, peering curiously at the bundle she carried. This was Mrs. Greig, wife of a government school teacher (she herself was a teacher), but the big attraction was her two-weeks old baby. "It's pretty little," somebody said.

"Well, I don't know," another of the *Bear's* sea-dogs commented. I've seen littler ones than this turn out to be bigger'n you. . . ."

"I expect we'd better get the baby inside," the mother said.

"Oh, yes, *ma'am!*" The anxious retinue folded by the wayside as the tiny passenger was gently carried below.

Happy mopped his brow. "Roundy-come-roundy! We sure get ourselves a bit of everything in the way of passengers."

"Makes it more interesting," I observed. The two teachers were outward bound after serving for three years among the Eskimos. I could not help but admire those stalwart souls who had given up so many of the usual comforts in order to bring the enlightenment of reading, writing, arithmetic, and general health training to those isolated people. The gear they had collected as momentoes was fantastic. Outstanding was a mastodon tusk, about ten feet long, which they had found fifty miles inland.

Near where the ivory tusk was lashed on deck stood

83

a huge Malamute dog who was chained to the pinrail of the foremast. He had come aboard like any other passenger for Nome and seemed quite frightened, although he did not bark, whine, or growl. When Happy walked up and cuffed his furry ears, the dog opened his mouth in a wide grin as if he were trying to laugh at us. There was nothing wrong with his appetite, though, for he gulped his dried fish with the gusto of a gourmand.

Looking down from the bridge now, Captain Cochran scowled into the wind. I had heard the Eskimos telling him of a change in the weather, and we ourselves had noted that the barometer was fluctuating nervously. It could mean anything, and even though there was not a sign of ice within miles, a good iceman could never forget what might happen. He could never let down his guard.

As the *Bear* stood out for deeper water, I dropped the canvas bucket overboard and filled it with seawater to test the temperature. This job had to be faithfully carried out, even as we sailed south. Our course lay straight for the middle of the pass between Little Diomede and Cape Prince of Wales, for time was pressing. The season was wearing on.

Steaming through the treacherous Bering Strait, currents swirled around us from many directions. Even in the darkness, we could feel them converging beneath us at that place where two continents reach out as if to touch one another. The evil lay in the fact that the currents were variable, depending on the sea, the wind, and the shape of the sea's bottom in the wider regions around.

Low-hanging fog fell heavier in the sky and enveloped the *Bear*. Disagreeable rain began dripping down, and I tightened the grip on my parka hood as I made my way along the deck. The long semilight evenings we had known in the high latitudes now deserted us, leaving a quick, oppressive blanket of darkness and gloom. It was strange and fearsome, and I wondered if I would ever get used to it. In the midst of all this, the Malamute dog began to howl in weird, mournful tones.

The wind sharpened from the southeast and began driving the pellets of rain into our faces. Soon it turned to sleet. By the middle of the eight-to-twelve watch, utter blackness enveloped everything. At each

The boy was to be tried for murder.

half-hourly striking of the ship's bell, the lookout at the masthead shouted, "All lights burning bright and no ships in sight!" We could not see him up there, nor he us, as he peered into the darkness.

The quartermaster took machine soundings each half hour at thirty fathoms, which was the expected depth of the water in the Strait. The wind increased to gale force, indicating we were beginning to lose the protection of Cape Prince of Wales, but the *Bear* kept slowly driving ahead. By this time the navigator's calculations put us almost through the Bering Strait, yet nobody could be sure because of the blackness which lay around us.

At midnight, the newly-called midwatch stumbled sleepy-eyed onto the deck. The old watch crawled dripping wet into their bunks. The new lookout aloft reported the brightness of the lights to the bridge. The new quartermaster went aft to take the first sounding of his watch. When he got it and looked at his reading, he made a wild rush to the bridge.

It was too late.

The *Bear* hit heavily on the bottom. Pandemonium broke loose.

Men came tumbling from their bunks as the vessel began thumping over the shoal, or whatever it was that we had struck.

"All hands! All hands!" roared Ralston, as he landed on his hands and knees in front of his bunk.

"All hands!" crackled the voice of John Lidmann from along the passageway.

The engine-room bells jangled. Bridge telegraphs clicked. Mr. Berg leaped out of the galley where he stood sipping a cup of hot coffee. Captain Cochran slid off the pilothouse emergency bunk where he had been napping. He leaped to the flying bridge with his shoestrings still dangling from his unlaced shoes.

Mr. Parker came running from the wardroom aft, half-clad. Mr. Perham, the inevitable pipe in his mouth, tramped down into the engine room. The officer of the watch began shouting orders; the quartermaster began walking the hand lead around the ship, attempting to feel the shape of the sea's bottom which we had so unexpectedly hit.

By this time, Mr. Berg was up in the linkings, like a shadow, working madly with his deck force to clear away the anchor gear. The carpenter feverishly turned

The Malamute dog grinned at Happy LaRue.

85

the steam valve at the capstan beside him. All the while, the wind whistled louder and the dog howled in panic. Now, the wind reached such force that it began to sing in the shrouds, like a ghostly reminder of old shipwrecks in these waters.

Mr. Parker relieved the officer of the watch. Captain Cochran shouted into the frantic din, "Let go the anchor, Mr. Parker!"

Then in a stentorian voice, half to the executive officer, half to the boatswain out on the forecastle head, he boomed, "Give it a short stay! We will swing around on the anchor under foot, Mr. Berg!"

The chain rattled down. The vessel lurched ahead and eased. The shoal was left behind, and the *Bear* rolled more evenly in the water now.

But the anchor did not hold!

"Five fathoms more, Mr. Berg!"

There was more rattle of the chain, then nothing. The head of the ship suddenly snubbed down into the sea as a bull would be snubbed to a tree stump. She veered off and began to swing . . . round and round through the cold, black water, seared white by its own turbulence.

I thought of the baby below, of its mother, and of the other passengers. What chance would they, or any of us, have if we didn't get ourselves out of this predicament?

To leeward, ugly white foam spat up out of the sea at us, and we knew this meant more rocks, more shoals. To the windward, there was only blackness, except for the ghostly whitecaps leaping at us from the night.

"Heave round, Mr. Berg!" The grumble of the capstan engine joined the shriek of the wind. The anchor came to a short stay, was broken out, and rose, dangling and mud-coated, to the surface of the water. The jangle of the engine-room bells told us the ship was moving ahead slowly. The deck force swung out the fishfall, and a man climbed down over the flare of the bow to hook on the anchor. The muddy hook was slowly brought to the rail.

Only now were we finally aware of the uproar below decks—a wild mixture of shouts and thuds. Suddenly I realized that ordinary seaman Gantley, a mere boy, who had been confined to the brig for breech of discipline, was pounding on the brig door and yelling

The ship was running clear again.

to get out. "Somebody unlock this door! Help! Help!"

The brig, located in the forehold below the water-line, was separated from the space used to stow spare sails. At the first pounding of the vessel, Gantley's two trouble-making buddies leaped from their bunks and raced through the confused berth deck, down the hatch to the main hold. Determined to free the prisoner, the two rough firemen seized the spare fire axes from a rack and began chopping down the door. But a spare sail had jammed against it. No one could get in—or out.

In the meantime, Ralston had obtained the brig keys from the officer of the deck and was close on their heels. "Barker! Whaley! Belay there or I'll have you all in the brig!" The emergency finally ended with Barker and Whaley still out of the brig, and Gantley still in.

The ship was running clear again. Tension eased off. Speechley, who at the call of "All hands" had hastened to his station in the engine room, now climbed up into the well deck, wiped his forehead with a sweat rag, and said, "Let's get some sleep, boys." He went forward and turned in for the second time within an hour.

Wet, half-asleep men gathered round the coffee pot, not quite sure whether to turn in again or stand by. The watch had been piped down, but the men preferred to stand around and talk over our narrow escape. The sea might get the *Bear,* but not this time.

The *Bear* steered southwest until she was well off-shore, then hauled into the original course. Checking the track back from Nome, the run of the log showed we had hit north of Cape Prince of Wales, that the current had slowed us down, and a cross current had set us to the eastward. It could have been disastrous; the ship struck at almost high water. If she had stayed aground an hour, it could have been fatal.

Captain Cochran spent the night pacing the deck, peering into the misty darkness. Time and again he fixed his eyes on the white, boiling water ahead. "Come right!" he would order. "Swing her left!" An added scowl settled over his features, his chin thrust out more sharply. There was not much talk on the bridge that night.

As I went about my duties, I wondered what thoughts flashed through the Bull Walrus' mind as he leaned into the wind, peering at the black nothing-ness ahead. Was he remembering the *Sea Ranger* which stranded on this same shoal years ago? The *Sea Ranger* was only a sailing ship and had no engines with which to take her off so she had broken up, her crew fleeing in small boats. By comparison, the *Bear's* plight was easy, yet Captain Cochran acted almost as if he had been hurt.

Why did he feel this way? Was it a matter of pride? The *Bear* was no different than other ships that had sailed these waters. Every cutter that came north had stranded at some time. The *Manning* had landed high and dry on a rock down in Shelikof Strait. The *Unalga* had stranded in Bristol Bay. The *Perry, Thetis, Corwin,* and *Rush* had all grounded. Nine-tenths of the ships that sailed into Alaskan waters stranded in some degree, and some of them, unfortunately, stayed stranded forever.

Yet, the grounding proved one thing. In spite of the inspection the previous year which had condemned the old ship as unseaworthy, her hull was still sound. She had not leaked a bucketful.

Septemeber 7, 1921. The season was getting old as the *Bear* steamed into Nome for the last time that year. The two bird hunters had stayed behind at Wainwright where they would winter over. Now, at Nome, we landed the teachers and their baby, the Malamute dog who had howled every night, the witnesses for the murder trial, and, last but not least, Mr. Watkins. I noticed the relief the Captain unsuccessfully tried to hide as the little man, complete with his book of magnetic data, instruments, and pup tent, climbed into the small boat and headed for shore. Mr. Watkins would go out in the *Victoria,* back to Washington, D. C., where he would work out the problems which had sent him afield.

The King Islanders who had spent the summer on the beach outside Nome had broken camp and were now waiting to get back to their island home eighty miles up the coast. The winds were picking up fresh again, this time out of the northwest, which would make them headwinds for the Eskimo umiaks.

"The *Bear* will take them home, bag and baggage," Captain Cochran said. This had been done for so long it was rumored that our skipper had been the first to start this practice. True or not, it made a good story.

Captain Cochran was no pompous martinet in his dealings with the Eskimos. Although he knew ships

and their strengths, and he understood about weather in the North, he was always willing to listen to those who knew more about it than he did. And he profited by the opinions of the Eskimos, who instinctively knew weather and ice.

During the summer, the King Islanders at Nome had turned their umiaks upside down on the beach and used them as houses. A few had tents. Now the boats, having been righted, were put to their regular use and brought their owners off *en masse.* Early in the morning of the propitious day, the villagers began breaking camp and bringing their possessions out to the ship. They came aboard like a drove of wild animals, yelling and shouting. Every child among them had an orange, or an apple, or a stick of gum held proudly in greasy hands, proof that the *Victoria* had just come in from the South with a load of the white man's delicacies. Skin boats were piled high on the quarterdeck. Next came the pots and pans, stoves, washtubs, pokes of oil, bedding, trunks, clothes of all sorts, washboards, lanterns, flour, canned goods, and even cornflakes. Following this came the highly prized "junk"; corrugated iron, ends of lumber, driftwood to be used as boat frames or piles for houses, empty gasoline tins, scrap iron, pieces of canvas, and rope ends. Anything that some ingenious Eskimo might find use for in the long, isolated winter was

89

Thor made friends with a King Island walrus hunter.

gathered up and brought along. After the large umiaks were hoisted and secured and the other boats secured, families found cozy spots for the trip home.

The King Islanders perched everywhere: on the forecastlehead, on the knighthead, even out in the basket (the netting spread out to catch the jib when being furled). The pilothouse was surrounded with them. They loitered aft on the poop deck and examined each part of the ship's equipment with great curiosity. They chattered constantly with one another. But it was no wonder that they had so much to say, for this was the most important single event of their year—going home.

It was a strange feeling to realize that we had the entire population of the island aboard the *Bear,* and what was more, it had increased since the early summer pilgrimage to Nome. New babies, and new pups, were part of our load, and the young ones outshrilled the chatter of the others.

Each woman soon found a corner for herself in which to crouch down and begin to sew. Most of them were making mukluks, the heels of which they crimped down with their teeth until their teeth were worn off. But they had long since given up their bone needles for steel ones, and they used heavy thread from the States instead of gut.

The umiaks came on board. Chockablock, they were hauled up under our lifeboats. Since there were seven skin boats and we had only five of ours, the remaining two umiaks would have to be trailed out astern. Or so we thought, but Captain Cochran would have none of it. "Mr. Parker," he said sternly, "I want all the boats clear of the water. Once we tried towing them. They got adrift and we nearly lost them."

No wonder the Eskimos worshipped the Bull Walrus! He knew what their boats meant to them. One of the two umiaks was hauled out of the water, canted on its side, and frapped against the *Bear's* hull. The other was hoisted on a whip at the foreyard and lashed, end up, to the shrouds. There, that ought to do it. The *Bear* was ready to go, loaded with Eskimos, dogs, gear, and boats. As the ship left Nome, the hubbub on deck slowly died away.

The dogs, exhausted from the long day of commotion, curled up to sleep. The men crawled under the boats or simply stretched out on the deck. Children

The Eskimos perched everywhere aboard the Bear.

flopped down in whatever space was left. But the women kept right on sewing, spreading their pieces of canvas or walrus hide for shelter against the wind. As it grew dark, they lit battered old lanterns and kept on working. A few of the men, not to be outdone by the energetic women folk, got busy with their trade, the intricate, never-ending carving of ivory.

Happy walked over and sat down on the edge of a life-jacket locker. There was a strange, faraway look in his eye, and I was sure of what he was thinking because he had so often expressed his thoughts to me in his peppery words: The frequent stops; the driving through the ice; the fighting against fog and currents to land and pick up passengers at outlandish places. There was all this, plus the tribulations of what many thought was poor food and facilities for the men and officers alike; the shortage of water; and now—prize insult of all—this taxi-service unlimited. The long voyage was now wearing on his nerves, as it was on all of us.

Seeing me studying his mood, he flung out his arms. "What's it all about? Why do perfectly normal people want to do *this* all their lives?"

It was not an easy thing to answer, because my thinking was so different from his. To me, the conditions which were obnoxious to others were the very reasons I had made this trip.

LaRue was thinking of the courage it took to endure all this. I was trying to soothe my thoughts with the lure, the history, and excitement of it all. I thought of the two bird hunters we had left behind at Wainwright to complete their collection. They would endure the sub-zero weather of the Arctic all winter long because of this lure. Mr. Watkins with his book of magnetic data had shared our own discomforts and privations in order to carry out his job and make his scientific contributions. Dr. Sturdevant—having pulled a multitude of teeth out of the blubber-eating mouths which stank as badly as the blubber they ate, having given endless pills, eased pains, and performed minor operations here and there where needed—would go home content that he had done his work properly. The King Islanders would go ashore to climb among their stilted huts and get ready to go out on the ice to hunt walrus, seals, and whales. They were well content that this mighty ship, the *Bear,*

guided by the king of captains, had brought them home. They were sure that he, or another captain, would do it again and again, as the years rolled by.

And lastly, the "king of the captains" would submit a report of his vessel's activities. The *Bear,* having embodied all these people and events, would wallow her way back over the ocean, concluding one more year of voyaging.

Well, thought I, as I watched Happy sitting there on the life-jacket locker, you surely did pose a mighty question when you asked what it was all about. I knew no better way of answering it than by just repeating, "Can you beat it?"

On the "plus" side of the ledger, we all had gathered souvenirs during the trip. Years later, when many of the annoying details of the Arctic voyage had been forgotten, we would have these treasures as memories. John Lidmann had been working at odd times on a dainty little ditty bag, a thing of fine workmanship with red, white, and blue herringbone stitches at the seams, a drawstring of square sennit with a handsome turk's-head knot in the circular bottom. Almost everybody had ivory of some sort— a cribbage board; a simple, clean tusk; or one with fish, seals, whales, and ships carved on it.

Some had feather parkas or mukluks, others had fox skins. One man had collected the skin from an unborn baby seal. I had the beautiful mukluks which Susie of Wainwright had made for me. And I had the Dutch Harbor journal, along with the key to room 27 of Ye Old Baranof Inn at Dutch Harbor, that place where whalemen had stopped to talk about whales and ice and Eskimos.

Sifting through my collection, I found a pair of hand irons from some ancient whale ship. These I had dug from a rubbish pile in Nome. But the best souvenir of all was the intense curiosity and enthusiasm which had been whipped up by my experiences. Some day, I vowed, I would get some of the bottom ironwood planking of the trader *Boxer* (for which a bay on St. Lawrence Island had been named) and make a ditty box out of it. I would one day get some white oak from the lobby of the Great Northern Hotel in Seattle where that rugged old

Kayaks were tied to the Bear *at King Island.*

93

Captain Tuttle of the *Bear* used to "come to anchor" for talk and companionship. I would make a sea chest of this wood to hold such mementoes as diaries and trinkets—all interlocked with memories.

In the early morning the *Bear* unloaded all the Eskimo passengers at King Island. We watched them dart toward shore in their deeply laden umiaks, singing, shouting as they paddled, while their mangy dogs growled and yelped their anger and enthusiasm.

"Well, that's that," announced Happy, seemingly glad to see them leave. But I noted a touch of sentiment in his voice as he called goodbye to them. Did he envy their primitive, simple existence in this far-off place? Would we ever meet any other humans with such naive trust in our every word? I doubted it.

Now the ship moved to St. Lawrence Island where at midnight we unloaded more gear, picked up mail, and let the natives aboard for their not-to-be-denied trading session. Then the anchor chain was shortened, ready to be broken out. I heard old John Lidmann, muttering out on the forecastlehead for the last time, that tune more than one man in the crew was singing to himself:

"Farewell, Arctic and Point Barrow, farewell,
  Norton Sound,
Greetings from a passing seaman, we are
  homeward bound.
Homeward bound it is, my boys, frap the
  boats in tight,
Set the topsails and the course and keep the
  lanterns bright."

But there was still one more task to do, to round out this voyage to the Far North. The *Bear* had to stop at the Pribilof Islands, the four little rocky points jutting out of the sea two hundred miles north of Unalaska. There were the famous seal rookeries, now protected by the government against indiscriminate slaughtering by seal poachers.

The *Bear* slowly crept across the darkening seas in the dense fog. In just such weather as this, years before, the cutter *Perry* had run aground. Finally, on the rocks abeam of us, we could see her rusty boilers, grim reminders of her fate.

94

The King Islanders were sorry to see us go.

The *Bear* glided safely in and came to anchor off the station on St. Paul Island. There were the lofty radio towers, a few white buildings, some unpainted shacks, excited people running along the shore and the superintendent of the station waiting on the small boat landing. "What are we putting in here for?" I asked John Lidmann.

"Over there," he pointed toward a warehouse, "are a hundred and fifty whiskey barrels filled with sealskins, salted down and ready to be shipped to the tannery at St. Louis."

I soon learned that each barrel contained fifty sealskins—seventy-five hundred sleek seals had died to fill those barrels. Big canvas boats built like umiaks soon brought the barrels out to the ship. We would have to load them fast, for the weather was changing and the surf was rising at the landing. Soon the ship was loaded and away we went to nearby St. George Island where we found more fog, more rocks, and, again, more natives running along the shore to greet us and more whiskey barrels filled with sealskins waiting to be shipped south. We were told that nineteen thousand skins were taken that year, to later adorn ladies of fashion in many parts of the world.

Some of us were more interested in the seals that were still alive than those salted down in the barrels. We watched the bull seals in their harems, roaring defiance to each other. Cows and their pups frisked in the water, examining the ship with great curiosity. These were the strange animals whose peculiar society and migrational habits had played a major role in the *Bear's* life.

Each year, between January and May, the entire seal herd moves south to the coastal waters of California. Each spring they move northward again, ignoring hundreds of miles of rocky coast, until they reach those barren islands called the Pribilofs. The bulls arrive a month ahead of the cows and set up their claims, fighting with each other continuously. This is when the "men are separated from the boys," that is, the old bulls chase all the younger, weaker males away to the other side of the rocks. The "bachelors" remain so until they find the courage and strength to challenge a full-grown bull for the right to establish a harem.

When the cows arrive, the bulls battle until every

The baby seals are playful creatures.

cow has been taken into a harem. During the breeding season, the pups conceived the year before are born. The bulls do nothing except fight and guard their harems, never eating during the entire time. Each cow nurses her own pup but will have nothing to do with a stranger, so if anything happens to a cow while she is hunting at sea, the pup slowly starves to death. Since a young seal cannot swim, much of the mother's time is spent in teaching her baby to survive in the water so it will be ready for the long journey south when the time comes.

As I watched the playful seals, my mind flicked back to the days when they were the unprotected victims of greedy hunters. Before the U. S. Coast Guard took over the duty of guarding their breeding grounds, the herds were hunted until they nearly became extinct. The story of those grim days was vividly told in Jack London's book, *Sea Wolf,* which described how Wolf Larsen lowered his boats among the herds of playful animals, blasted them with shotguns, and then disappeared into the mists before patrol vessels could overtake them. Those were the days of racing and chasing, cursing and fighting, among crews of Japanese, Russians, Canadians, and Americans—rugged adventurers all—who wantonly killed the seals for their valuable, and forbidden, pelts.

Yes, those were bloody times, filled with rovers, thieves, and pirates, and their desperate battles with the elements, pursuit by hovering men-o'-war, and an occasional sudden end by shipwreck. Traces of those days still remained—the rusting iron of the wrecked cutter *Perry* on the nearby beach; deserted lookout towers overlooking the seal rookeries; the lonely graves of marauders who had died in pitched battles; and, sometimes, a rusting wreck of a ship.

In 1910 the cutter *Perry* was cruising among the sealing schooners, mostly Japanese, which hovered outside the three-mile limits off the Pribilofs, like flies around a sugar bowl. The patrol went on endlessly, as Coast Guardsmen boarded the ships, searched them, and constantly checked their positions to make sure that they stayed outside the restricted waters. And then, early one foggy morning, the *Perry* went aground. Her crew labored frantically to get the ship afloat. They sent down the yards, struck the topmasts, jettisoned heavy gear, but finally had to give up in despair. A radio distress call brought the cutters *Tahoma* and *Manning* to the rescue, and the *Perry* was abandoned and left to break up and rust away. Eleven years later, all we could see of her were her rusting boilers.

In those days, the smaller sealing schooners carried from ten to fifty men in their crews. They worked three men in a boat, two hunters and a boat steerer. Indians preferred spears, but the white men used rifles and shotguns. When a sealer came upon a herd, it lowered its boats, which scattered like dogs on the hunt. Often boats got out of sight of the mother ship. Winds came up, fog came in, sea and wind drove them to leeward. Boats might be lost for days, sometimes to be picked up by another sealer, sometimes to disappear forever. Sometimes the sealing ships themselves sank, or smashed up on unexpected rocks. The old records are filled with accounts of these disasters. "Lost, with all hands" was a common notation, especially during seasons of strong gales. And one might add, "Lost, with all skins," for often the ships went down with the entire season's catch.

It was all different now. The seals were killed under strict government control. Even so, it was a gruesome business, but probably no more so than any necessary slaughtering of animals for the use of man. Only the bachelors were killed for their furs, because they were not needed for the continuation of the herd. The barking, frisking animals were herded to the killing grounds, where Aleut killers walked among them swinging baseball-bat clubs. The air was filled with the frenzied barking of seals and the shouts of the Aleuts working quickly, stabbing each stunned seal and skinning it on the spot, until the allotted number were killed for the day.

The last barrel of skins was hauled on board and lashed down. There was an imperceptible sigh amongst the crew of the *Bear* as this final chore was completed. The stopover had been necessary, and we all recognized the fact that somebody had to do it. Yet, once we had turned around at Demarcation Point and begun the homeward passage, a kind of involuntary urgency seemed to speed all our actions. We had sailed North to see what was up there, and now our curiosity was satisfied. Everyone now had the same thought in his mind—"Let's get back."

Even the Captain was losing his patience. I studied him as he leaned over the railing, peered through his binoculars, and swung them around as if to study the weather. To him, the loading of sealskins was far less challenging than breaking through the ice.

The oilskin-clad Aleuts chattered as they loaded the final bit of cargo. Captain Cochran paced the quarterdeck with noticeable irritation. Each delay in loading only aggravated him. Thor seemed to take on the irritation of his master. The dog raced around the quarterdeck, whining as if he would lose his mind. Lately he had been having fits and was allowed on deck only if he was accompanied by the cabin boy.

At last the *Bear* turned her stern to the fogbound islands. Across two hundred miles of green, murky waters, Cape Cheerful lay ahead. As the ship crawled along over the seemingly endless expanse of sea, with a leaden sky hanging above her, the sullen men fretted and Captain Cochran seemed to be slowly reaching the boiling point from his own pressure. His orders were more curt, his responses more impatient. His reindeer coat had become worn and frayed at the edges during the summer, and now his nerves were also frayed. Gone were the time-killing talks, the stories of old wrecks and disasters. It was no nonsense from now on in, and we were "tightened up" as never before. The officers felt it, the crew felt it, we almost suspected the ship felt it. And the very tenor of the ship took on the character of her stern, exasperated Captain.

"Cape Cheerful ahead!" shouted John Lidmann from the crow's nest. Although it was only a low, dark line on the horizon, the sight had a magical effect on all of us. Staring at it, entranced, we saw it as the embodiment of our dreams, a symbol of things which were real and suddenly very dear to us. Cape Cheerful! At last I realized how it came by its name, thanks to Captain Cook.

Soon the *Bear* came up with a little steam whaler, still bright and new, out of Akutan station. Now we could watch a whale hunt. All across the Bering Sea, we had watched the great beasts floating calmly in our

99

path, as if they knew our business was other than whales. I trembled to think of how men used to hunt them down in an open boat, with only a harpoon for a weapon, when one blow of their huge flukes could smash a boat to kindling wood. Now the whale hunters used a steam engine to catch the whale, and a gun to kill him. The sturdy little ship went after its prey almost like a bull terrier after a mastiff. Maneuvering closer, we could see it skimming over the sea. Suddenly, a puff of white leaped out from the bow. A faint murmur drifted over the water and we recognized the boom of a whale gun.

Closer now, we could see that the harpooner had hit his target. The whale surged away, tightening the line which held him fast to the whaler, and the tug-of-war began. So intrigued were we at this exciting spectacle that we very nearly forgot our own precarious position. There, ahead of us, was a large school of whales forging right across our bow like a fleet of ships. There were dozens of them, moving, swirling, thrashing up the water as they followed their pilot.

For the next fifteen minutes, the *Bear* found herself winding in and out among them, changing course from time to time to avoid running them down. The whales swam unconcernedly around us. By the time we had cleared them, we had come almost alongside the tiny whaler and could see her working with her newest catch. Soon she would have it surfaced, blown up with air, and be off on another chase. Off to leeward, we could see a small red flag bobbing in the sea, indicating that another whale had been buoyed and was ready to be picked up at the end of the hunt.

Later, while we roamed the beach at Unalaska, we went to Akutan station to see the whales hauled out, waiting to be cut up and turned into whale oil. What trackless seas had they swam in their long journeys, almost from pole to pole, what wonders had they seen in the green depths where no man went? Had they too reached an Ultima Thule—some distant land saved only for Leviathans—or was this what whales were meant for, to stink and bloat in the sun while seagulls picked lice off their dead backs and men cooked them up for oil? Looking at their huge bodies, more like submarines than animals, one could almost wish the harpoon gun had missed.

But the harpoon gunner seldom missed. As the *Bear*

We wished the harpoon guns had missed.

moved on toward Unalaska, the gun boomed again. Another dead whale, another red flag.

"Well, that makes quite a finale to our trip, doesn't it?" Happy beamed for the first time in hours. The experience had the same effect throughout the ship. Everyone had been lifted from deep depression to an ecstasy as high as the clouds. Captain Cochran came out of his sullen half. His eyes sparkled with interest and amusement again. The thrill of the chase, though it was not his own, had wrought magic. I had the feeling that now I knew the thoughts of Herman Melville as he sat down to write *Typee*. Into our faces blew the same sonorous winds that Captain Ahab had faced across green and purple seas in quest of Moby Dick. What had been the goal of those lost souls he lived among? There was a haven each of them longed for, even though in the grime of toil each saw it in a different light. No matter what our individual feelings in the matter, the *Bear* would take us all to the same port. So be it; the *Bear* passed on into Illiuliuk Bay and headed for Unalaska.

"From ice breaking to mountain climbing! Now, that's quite a change, if you ask me." Happy had just agreed to climb Mount Ballyhoo with me for a look at the view of Dutch Harbor and the surrounding country. The climb was well worth the effort, for the view from the top, nearly 3,000 feet high, was spectacular. Looking northward, we could see bug-like dots on the sea, which we knew were steam whalers from Akutan searching for whales.

In the crude little hut on the mountain we found a visitors' book, where we promptly scribbled our names, along with the name of our ship. And then we sat down on a rock and talked, swapping more tales of truth and fiction, dreaming a bit as we drank in the beauty of the scene. "Sea dogs chewing at old bones of adventure," I thought to myself. Always curious, always questioning, always wanting to know who did what and why.

While the *Bear* lay in Dutch Harbor, we had time out to explore the beaches, the harbor, and even the graveyards. The beach was literally lined with fascinating objects of Alaskan history. We passed the Jesse Lee Home for Aleut children, with its attached

Back at Dutch Harbor. Unalaska is in the foreground, Mount Ballyhoo looms in the background.

hospital for the care of sick and injured people from outlying regions. Dr. Newhall, the chief missionary in charge, was also a practicing physician and did all the needed surgery.

As we passed some old Russian cannon, Happy laughed, "Look at that. Cowboys and Indians!" I too was amused to see Aleut boys straddling a cannon in some childish, wild west game. Nearby, we watched Indian dogs fighting over the carcasses of salmon which they had dragged from Unalaska Creek.

We had time on this last stroll before boarding the *Bear* to have a few parting words with friends in Dutch Harbor—the old postmaster, Mr. Finch; the deputy collector of customs, Mr. Bulshanin; and the U. S. marshal, Mr. Bucknell.

Farther along the beach we watched the schooner *Everett Hayes* being readied to haul out of the water so that her skipper, Mr. Gore, could see what damage had been done when he rubbed her keel over a shoal out to the westward. Happy whispered to me, "That old rascal is suspected of smuggling illegal sea otter skins." Later, we would hear that the schooner had hit another rock, running down from Attu, and sank with a load of blue fox skins.

Finally, we passed the house where an old Aleut woman called "Rock of Ages" lived. This old woman, whose age could not even be guessed, was one of the best basket weavers from Attu. She had brought in her season's work to be sold while she spent the winter in Unalaska.

And then we were back at the dock where the *Bear* and the *Unalga* lay. John Lidmann hung to the weather upper topsail yardarm of the *Bear,* prying out the head-earing of a clean, new sail which Hans Berg had hauled from the locker to replace the smoke-begrimed sail the *Bear* had carried all summer.

"How do you like our 'Homeward Bound' sail?" he called. A tingle of excitement swept over me as I realized the *Bear* was about to set sail again. There was much work to be done, however, before we could get under way. Coal would have to be brought aboard from the *Unalga,* and while this was being done a delegation of Jesse Lee Home children looked on with fascination. We waved to them from time to time, rather pleased to have such an admiring audience.

Finally, the coaling was finished. Again we washed away the dust, covered the hatches, hoisted the boats, and secured them for sea. And in all the excitement, while mongrel Aleut dogs ashore ran around the dock, barking, fighting, and snatching bits of meat and bones from the garbage cans, poor old Thor had his last fit and died in the cabin bathtub. There would be no more sounds of frightened whimpering as the *Bear* lurched and rolled with the swells. There would be no more calls of "Dog on the Q.D.!" The dog who had never wanted to go to sea in the first place was sent ashore for the last time.

A group of sailors lined the rail to watch as two of the crew, one carrying a shovel and one carrying the dead dog, crossed the dock to bury Thor at the edge of Unalaska Creek. I glanced at Captain Cochran as he stood near the gangway. No emotion showed on his face, yet I noticed he was unable to talk with the man standing next to him.

At that moment, even the man who had hated the Captain's dog could only feel sorry for the Captain.

Chapter Sixteen : Seattle in the Morning!

Homeward bound!

I stood on the flying bridge, rolling the wheel right and left as the *Bear* steamed out around Tuscarora Reef. To port lay Dutch Harbor dock and Molly's House. To starboard was Priest Rock, still painted white. At the Dutch Harbor dock I could see the *Algonquin*. We had last seen her at the seal islands. Where, if ever, would I see her again? I was reminded of the first time I had seen and boarded her; how often I had crossed her bows since then, as if inexorably we were tied together in some way.

Unalga Pass opened on our starboard beam now, boiling white, not a safe way to get out into the Pacific. The *Bear* continued on to Akutan Pass and headed through, even here finding white water on both sides of us. Once clear of the reef, we found a fresh westerly breeze ready to drive us homeward.

There is always elation in a homeward-bound trip, but as I lay in my bunk that night I felt a certain sense of frustration, too. Was my long struggle to sail in this old hulk, which now rocked me back and forth unsympathetically, to be just another escapade? Was it merely a dribbling away of time and effort? Was it an escape, to be followed by more escapes until there was no significance in a journey such as this?

I lay behind my bunk curtain and tried to figure out the answer. I pressed my shoulder against the ship-side bulkhead to steady me against the roll of the sea and gripped at the timbered brace over my pillow.

Above my head were old boards, layers of paint, scars cut by men who had slept there years before.

Above my head, feet thumped on deck. Hundreds, thousands of feet had thumped along that same deck in the past half century. Most of them were gone now—they were only phantom feet in the night, a dim part of my fancy. In the very bunk where I lay, many men had lain before. And in all the battered old wooden bunks around me, many other men had lived and slept in other days; the rough, the tough, the braggarts, the shy, the stolid, the panicky, the ship carvers, and those who tied fancy knots and wove sennit baskets. All had served and passed along.

If now I should step out from behind the curtain of my bunk, would the fancy become as real as those feet which were at the moment pounding the deck above my head? Each of those ghostly men had set out to find something. And the men who commanded them—Hooper, Healy, Tuttle, Cochran—had also been searching for something. Each of the leaders would scowl and growl his way along but none could destroy what was living inside him, that something that had to come alive for him or his voyaging would be futile. I was trying to make that something come alive for me, but would I ever succeed?

Somehow I hoped to find the answer in Captain Cochran who now slept aft. Yet, even as I had watched him and listened to his words of advice and command throughout the long voyage, he remained a stranger, a strict old man with a job to do. Not once had he let down the curtain from around his soul to show fully what lay inside him.

But wait! My mind flashed to a few hours earlier. The old Bull Walrus had stood on the bridge and watched the shoulder of Akutan Island fade over the quarter of the *Bear*. I had seen him sigh with relief as if the weight of the world were lifted from his shoulders. There would be no more Alaskan rocks to worry about from now on. Good, deep ocean lay ahead. "Well, that's that," he'd said with a festive smile, the first I'd seen on his weathered face. "I'm turning in."

Thinking of this, I suddenly felt a release of my tense emotions. There was an answer after all, and it came with bounding joy. It was so simple I wondered why I had tortured myself in the search for it. I had cleaved the Gordian knot clear through. I had been to Thule in my own small and unimportant way. But to me it was all important, and a tight knot of satisfaction came to my throat as I realized this. Whatever might come later could never change the fact that I had been to Thule. I might chop-chop in a rickshaw down Bubbling Wells Road in old Shanghai, or go rolling down to Rio, or fly post-haste over the Casbahs along the shores of the ancient Barbary Coast. But none of those could bring a greater joy than I now felt.

For I had been. Yes, that was it. I had made the trip, and now I was coming back.

As I lay and listened to the creak of the *Bear's* sturdy timbers, heard the clatter of feet on deck above me, the whine of brace blocks, and the sound of Boatswain Berg's voice in the night calling, "Square the foreyard! Overhaul the topsail braces!" I knew that the wind was fair. It was urging us on to Seattle at last. I went to sleep, finally, while phantom feet danced on deck, and the ghosts of all the *Bear's* old crews sang in the night.

> "Seattle in the morning, boys,
> Seattle in the morning. . . ."

Seattle! Ships from all over the world sailed through

"Seattle in the morning, boys, Seattle in the morning. . . ."

the island-dotted reaches of Puget Sound and into Elliott Bay. Tall buildings loomed against the skyline as we steamed up to the Bell Street dock. The *Bear* looked smaller and more weather-beaten than ever, in the company of freshly painted Navy ships and gleaming liners.

Captain Cochran resumed his irritated manner as the crew, in eagerness to do things right, seemed to do everything wrong. While we were shouting, "Hurray, we're home!" he was grumbling, "What's the matter with the engine room? Why are they so slow?" The quartermaster was slow at the helm. Even the men on the dock were slow taking in the lines. To make matters more annoying, the wind off the bay held the ship away from the pier and the eddying current ran contrary.

At last the lines were doubled up, the engines secured, and the watch piped down. A sigh of relief escaped each of us as the Bull Walrus stamped down off the bridge. "Mr. Parker," he said gruffly, "I'll be going ashore now."

So would everyone else who could possibly manage it. Many of the men would be paid off in the morning, and I could not help but remember the Captain's vow to make sailors of them. He had done just that with a crew who grumbled as loud as the worst but nevertheless turned into fine seamen. When the new recruits came aboard on the next trip, there would be oldtimers on hand to make them into sailors, too.

The *Bear* would sail on to San Francisco, but I was to be paid off in Seattle. On my last eight-to-twelve watch in the old ship, as I stood by the gangway, I mulled the whole experience over in my mind. I had other places I wanted to go, other ships to see. I had best make the break before I became too attached to the *Bear,* turned into a plank owner.

The night wind blew briskly out of the southwest, the air was squally. The tide was out, all eighteen feet of it, and the *Bear* hung low on her lines, surging back and forth in the eddy caused by the wind and the swell from a passing tug. I breathed in the tangy salt air with satisfaction as I thought once more of my cruise. I had sailed in the *Bear.* I had been a part of her, to the top of the world and back, to Ultima Thule and back. The dream had come true.

At midnight, down the dock came John Lidmann, the old sailor whose own world of the sea churned within his rugged soul. He was returning to the only home he knew, the *Bear,* murmuring some half-remembered, half-forgotten song as he swayed along. He had had his run on the beach, and would be ready to settle down to work in the morning.

Along came Paddy, strutting like a grenadier, his feet not quite sure of their way in the darkness, but his spirit glowing. Along came someone singing happily "Blast me eyes, the ship's a-sinking!" Along came Happy, growling his old lament and chanting his joys as before: "Now hear this! She's the greatest ship in the world, the best-feeding ship that ever came down from the North, and we're having ham and eggs for breakfast in the morning!"

So they came back to the ship during the night, the older men perhaps a little more silent, the younger ones yelling a little louder. Steady Chuck Speechley had long since turned in. The return from Alaska was nothing new to him. But with Crandall it was different. He was anxious to get ashore. He would be paid off, only to fade away into that indefinite world of the roving sailor, to go where the wind willed.

Out of the wardroom stepped Mr. Parker, for a stroll on deck before turning in. He would be the officer who signed my discharge in the morning. "Goodnight," he said pleasantly before going below. It was hard to realize we would not be shipmates again. Soon, Captain Cochran returned on board, his face appearing high in the night as he gripped the hand rail where the gangway now slanted down at a 45 degree angle to the deck below. "Quartermaster!" he called down. "Quartermaster, steady the gangway." He came down the steep gangway like a sailor coming down from aloft, turned, nodded his approval, mumbled something that sounded like, "Thank you, quartermaster. Goodnight," and disappeared into the cabin hatch.

Then it was I became filled with a sense of being a part of that old ship. By the magic of association I had been accepted into a fraternity of the sea. I had become shipmates with a legion of men, in a rare relationship, one of the *Bear's* men.

The clouds broke away then, and the light of the autumn moon touched the shining brass of the old bell marked "Secor and Co., 1838" which had marked the time so long for other ships and was now tolling it for the *Bear*. It would toll again at the change of the watch at midnight. The wind sang its own tales of mystic adventures from the top-hamper above. The swell of the harbor waters sounded like muted voices, discussing old times. The *Bear* stirred, and I heard the creak of her hull as it rubbed against the pilings of the dock. Can a ship speak? Does a ship ever say goodbye?

Goodbye, old ship!

Yet, I did not want to say goodbye to her, nor to the men, nor to the Captain who sailed her, because goodbyes are such final things. The Captain was no longer that "old Bull Walrus" of forecastle banter, but a remarkable shipmate. I was certain I could not say goodbye to my memory of him, nor to his words "Strike the bell eight, Sir," which he had so often said, nor least of all to the *Bear*.

So, when midnight came, I tapped eight bells for the last time in this ship I was about to leave behind, turned the watch over to my relief, went below, and turned in.

In the morning I would put my seabag over my shoulder, say "So long" to the watch on deck, and walk down the gangway and away. I knew I would not look back at the *Bear*. I had learned that a sailor should never say "Goodbye."

Goodbye, old ship!

From 1874 to 1884 the Bear *was based in St. John's, Newfoundland, as a part of the Grieve sealing fleet.*

In February, 1884, she was purchased by the U. S. Consul and fitted out as a rescue ship to search for the Greely Expedition.

In 1885 the ship was taken over by the U. S. Revenue Service. She sailed from Staten Island on November 8, 1885, and reached San Francisco on February 23, 1886.

On April 21, 1886, the Bear *was at the Pribilof Islands to search for the crew of the bark* Amethyst. *For the next thirty-nine years the* Bear *made annual Arctic trips. Her annual patrols ceased in September, 1925.*

In 1929 the ship was decommissioned and taken over by the City of Oakland, California.

In 1932, the ship was purchased by Rear Admiral Richard E. Byrd, U.S.N., for an expedition to the Antarctic. She sailed to the Atlantic, was refitted at the Boston Navy Yard, sailed south on September 25, 1933, and reached Bay of Whales, Antarctica, on January 31, 1934.

The Bear *was commissioned by the U. S. Navy in 1939, and decommissioned on June 9, 1944. In February, 1948, she was sold by the U. S. Maritime Commission to a private purchaser in Canada.*

The ship sank while under tow from Nova Scotia to Philadelphia, March 19, 1963.

Young Ransom joined the Bear *at* **Unalaska.**

Dutch Harbor *was the haunt for warships, cutters, sealers, salmon packets, and merchant ships alike.*

Nunivak Island, *off the mouth of the* **Kuskokwim River,** *was the* Bear's *first landfall in the Bering Sea.*

The King Islanders made their summer headquarters at **Nome.**

The Bear *brought* **St. Michael** *its first mail of the year.*

In **Golovnin Bay,** *the ship took fresh water out of the snow rivers, and then headed westward across* **Norton Sound** *towards* **St. Lawrence Island,** *where Paddy went ashore to shoot reindeer.*

King Island *is a lonely, mist-shrouded rock discovered and named by Captain Cook.*

The photograph on the jacket was made at **Emma Harbor** *in 1921.*

The Chukchis live at **Providence Bay.**

At **Whalen** *Silverman the trader came on board.*

The Bear *then proceeded to* **East Cape** *to take the stricken* Maud *in tow.*

Kotzebue Sound *was discovered by Otto Kotzebue in 1816.*

Icy Cape *was reached by Captain Bligh while seeking the Northwest Passage.*

Cape Prince of Wales *is the point of Alaska which is nearest Siberia.*

At **Wainwright,** *Susie requested a letter from the "outside."*

Point Barrow *is the northernmost tip of continental United States.*

The whaleship Reindeer *was crushed in the ice at* **Cross Island** *in 1894.*

Demarcation Point *marks the boundary line between Alaska and Canada.*

Herschel Island *is fifty miles to the east.*

The Bear *loaded sealskins at* **St. Paul Island** *in the* **Pribilofs.**

Unimak Pass *is the main passage between the Pacific and the Bering Sea.*

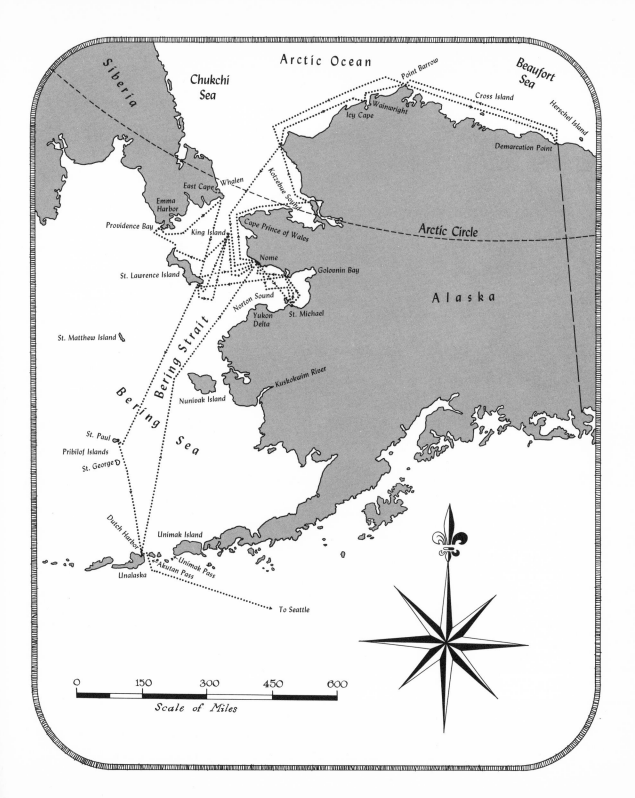

Siberia

Chukchi
Sea

Arctic Ocean

Beaufort
Sea

Point Barrow

Cross Island

Wainwright

Icy Cape

Herschel Island

Demarcation Point

East Cape

Whalen

Kotzebue Sound

Emma
Harbor

Arctic Circle

Providence Bay

King Island

Cape Prince of Wales

Nome

Alaska

Golovnin Bay

St. Lawrence Island

Norton Sound

St. Michael

Yukon
Delta

St. Matthew Island

Bering Strait

Kuskokwim River

Bering Sea

Nunivak Island

St. Paul

Pribilof Islands

St. George

Dutch Harbor

Unimak Island

Unalaska

Akutan Pass

Unimak Pass

To Seattle

0   150   300   450   600

Scale of Miles

113

United States Coast Guard Cutter Bear

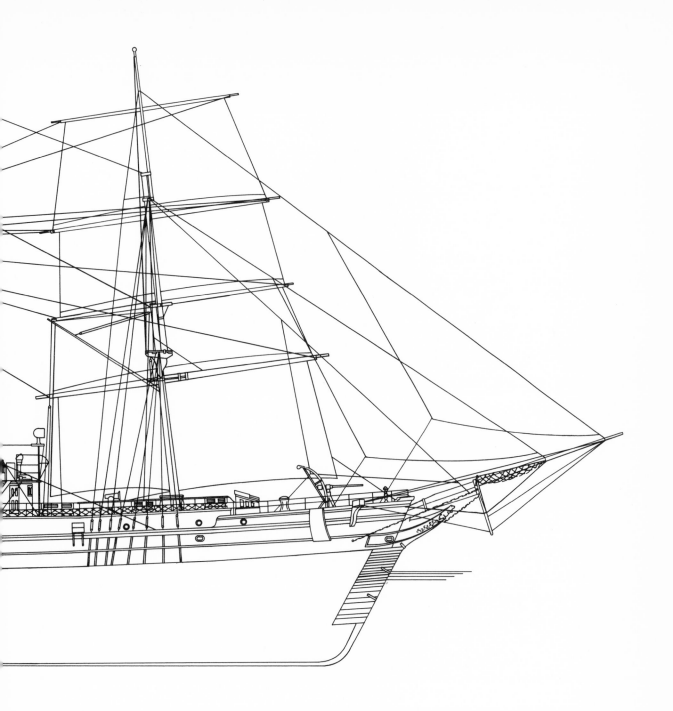

0   10   20   30   40   50

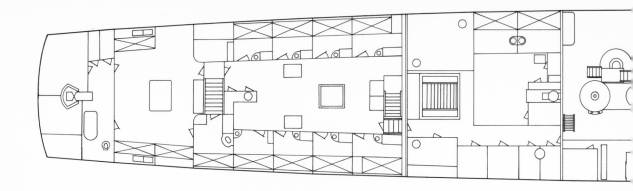

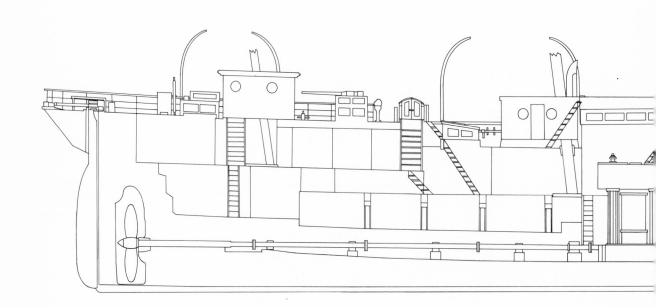

Specifications:

Built by Alexander Stephen & Sons, Dundee, Scotland, 1873–74.

Over-all length: 198'6", Length at waterline: 190'4", Beam: 29'9", Draft: 18'8", Displacement: 1,700 tons, Barkentine rig: foremast square rigged; mainmast and mizzenmast fore-and-aft rigged, Power plant: coal-fired, single-ended Scotch boiler with working pressure of 70 pounds. Two-cylinder compound engine (26" x 50" x 30") developing 500 indicated horsepower. Speed: 9 knots.

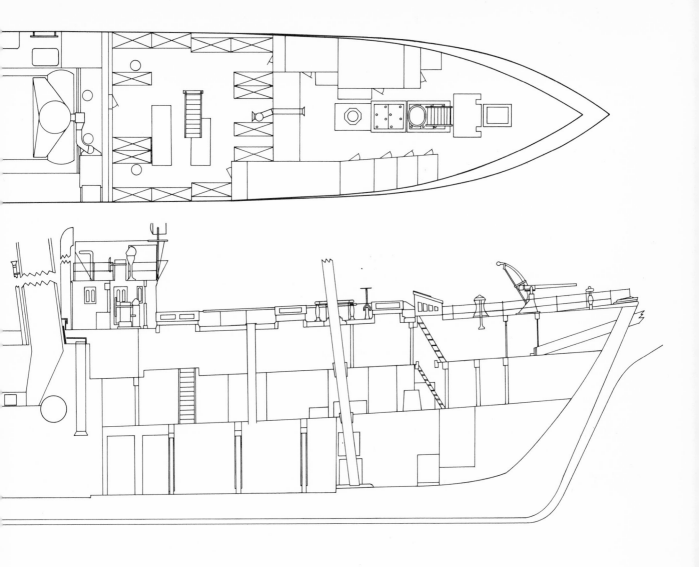

Hull of six-inch-thick strakes of oak bolted to Scottish oak ribs with Swedish iron. Decks of teakwood. Side sheathing of Australian iron bark. Bottom of yellow pine. Foremast and mizzenmast of Norway pine, mainmast of hollow iron. Bow specially reinforced with heavy oak timbers for working in ice.

Plans for a scale model of this ship may be obtained from the Smithsonian Institution, Washington, D.C.

117

Suggested Reading List

Anderson, William R. *First Under the North Pole* (World Publishers, 1959).

Barber, Noel. *Adventures at Both Poles* (Heinemann, 1963).

Bixby, William. *Race to the South Pole* (McKay, 1961).

Euller, John. *Arctic World* (Abelard, 1958).

Fairley, T. C. and C. Israel. *True North* (St. Martins, 1957).

Francis, Henry S. and P. M. Smith. *Defrosting Antarctic Secrets* (Coward—McCann, 1962).

Frank, R., Jr. Frozen Frontier: *The Story of the Arctic* (Crowell, 1961).

Frank, R., Jr. Ice Island: *The Story of Antarctica* (Crowell, 1957).

Horizon (periodical). *Heroes of Polar Exploration* (American Heritage, 1963).

London, Jack. *Sea-Wolf* (Grosset, 1916).

Ogle, Edward. *Getting to Know the Arctic* (Coward—McCann, 1963).

Rapaport, Stella F. *The Bear, Ship of Many Lives* (Dodd, Mead, 1962).

Smith, Frances C. *World of the Arctic* (Lippencott, 1960).

Stefansson, Evelyn. *Here is the Far North* (Scribner, 1957).

Sullivan, Walter. *White Land of Adventure* (McGraw—Hill, 1957).

M. A. Ransom first joined the Coast Guard in 1919, for a year's duty. He stayed on to serve another year, during which time the trip in the *Bear* was made.

He re-enlisted again in 1923, and was commissioned in 1924. During his service with the Coast Guard, from seaman up through Lieutenant Commander, he served in ten different vessels on both coasts, from the Arctic to Mexico, and from New England to the Rio Grande. He also had four years of duty on the Great Lakes. He saw duty in the *Haida* in the Bering Sea in 1924 when that vessel escorted the U. S. Army's World Flight Aviators for a month before they took off for the Kuriles.

Since his retirement in 1947, he has devoted his time to research on Coast Guard vessels and personnel, naval history, and sea lore. He has been a contributor to the *U. S. Naval Institute Proceedings.*

A picture of Lieutenant Commander Ransom, as a seaman at the time the *Bear* visited Demarcation Point in 1921, appears on page 75.

Eloise Katherine Engle was born in Seattle, Washington, and as a child often went aboard sailing ships in Puget Sound. She is married to Captain Paul R. Engle, (MC)U.S.N. and, as a Navy wife, has traveled extensively. They have three children.

Members of her family live in Alaska, and Alaska and the waters in which the *Bear* sailed are well-known to Mrs. Engle. Her husband had duty aboard ship at Dutch Harbor during World War II.

Mrs. Engle began her writing career with work on newspapers in Hawaii and Guam. It was while living in Guam that she wrote her first book, an account of Magellan's voyage around the world. She has since had a number of successful young-adult books published.

The text of this book is set in ten point Granjon, with two points of leading. The chapter titles are eighteen point Garamont italic.

The book is printed in offset on Ticonderoga text paper, Colonial White. The cloth is Columbia Lynnbrook Black, LNV-1750, natural finish.

Design by Gerard Valerio.

Editorial production by Louise Gerretson.

The book was composed and printed by The John D. Lucas Printing Company, Baltimore, Maryland.

The book was bound by Moore & Company, Baltimore, Maryland.